Inspiration FROM THE Garden

DEVOTIONS FOR GROWING IN FAITH

EDITORS OF GUIDEPOSTS

Guideposts

A Gift from Guideposts

Thank you for your purchase! We want to express our gratitude for your support with a special gift just for you.

Dive into ***Spirit Lifters***, a complimentary e-book that will fortify your faith, offering solace during challenging moments. Its 31 carefully selected scripture verses will soothe and uplift your soul.

Please use the QR code or go to **guideposts.org/spiritlifters** to download.

Inspiration from the Garden

Published by Guideposts
100 Reserve Road, Suite E200
Danbury, CT 06810
Guideposts.org

Cover design by Juicebox Designs
Cover illustration by Kristi Smith
Typeset by Aptara, Inc.

ISBN 978-1-961442-34-4 (softcover)
ISBN 978-1-961442-35-1 (epub)

Printed and bound in the United States of America
10 9 8 7 6 5 4 3 2 1

Connection with gardens, even small ones, even potted plants, can become windows to the inner life. The simple act of stopping and looking at the beauty around us can be prayer.

—Patricia R. Barrett, *The Sacred Garden*

INTRODUCTION

The Lord *will guide you always; he will satisfy your needs in a sun-scorched land and will strengthen your frame. You will be like a well-watered garden, like a spring whose waters never fail.*

—Isaiah 58:11 (NIV)

Gardening dates back to ancient times, when plants were used for food, medicine, and other practical purposes. Although gardening has evolved in numerous ways, the popularity of modern gardening remains—and not just as a means to provide nourishing food and glorious flowers.

Each of the writers in *Inspiration from the Garden* agrees that gardens and the natural world can both delight *and* instruct us, providing spiritual lessons no matter what season we're in. The heartfelt, personal devotions in these pages reflect on the hope, comfort, and peace that gardening has provided them.

Read about what it means to be nurtured, pruned, and watered by God. The writers gently explain that there is a time to plant and a time to uproot, both in their garden beds and in their lives. And they underscore, again and again, the fact that growth takes time. Just as gardens delight our senses by their variety, the readings in this book offer an array of spiritual insights and perspectives. From the joy of discovering seedlings sprouting from the earth to the delight of the sweet fragrance of a rosebush in bloom to the challenge of pulling stubborn weeds, these writers transform ordinary, everyday moments into fodder for deep reflection. They look with openness and curiosity at the way the natural world grows and thrives—and how this echoes the way God is working in their lives.

Whether you like to get your hands dirty or simply admire the beauty of gardens and nature from afar, each day's message will remind you that God is always growing something new in your life—even in the seasons when you can't yet see it.

—Editors of Guideposts

SOWING SMALL PRAYERS

"For the eyes of the Lord are on the righteous and his ears are attentive to their prayer."—1 Peter 3:12 (NIV)

Hesitation swelled in my spirit. Despite my training to become a certified master naturalist, I didn't know how my kids and I were going to plant a pollinator garden. Trying to recall the names of plants native to our Colorado soil scrawled across my notebook pages, I came up short.

Months ago, the idea of a native pollinator garden popped into my head and quickly transformed into a prayer. It seemed a small thing, one that the Lord might not care about. Surely He has bigger causes to tend to than a ten-by-twenty-foot plot of dirt, right?

Yet before spring's thaw, an email dropped into my inbox with the subject line: "Order Your Garden in a Box Today!" Intrigued, I opened it. A local organization was offering boxed kits of young plants.

I browsed the catalog and prayed silently, "Thank You, Lord!" when I saw the "Colorado Oasis" garden, displaying a beautiful array of native plants providing pollen for our insects and birds.

Soon we'd pick up our seedlings, a step-by-step guide to each plant, and a design map for how to arrange them. It was precisely the help and confidence I needed to step into this unfamiliar soil—the same fertile ground where God is growing my "small prayers" into greater faith.

Lord, You hear and answer every "small prayer" in Your timing. Help me to trust You with every care on my heart, no matter the size.

—Eryn Lynum

GROWING IN FAITH

What is a dream or concern that feels too insignificant for you to "bother" God with? Write it down and pray over it each day this week.

EDEN EXEMPLIFIED

He defends the cause of the fatherless and the widow, and loves the foreigner residing among you, giving them food and clothing. —Deuteronomy 10:18 (NIV)

It was a handmade sign that first led me to Maureen's farm. "For Sale—Maple Syrup," it read.

I had been driving along the Maine back roads leading to our summer cabin. Turning into the dirt driveway by the sign, I rounded a curve and encountered a modest clapboard farmhouse. To my right were the most exquisite garden beds I had ever seen. Clusters of giant ripe tomatoes seemed to burst off plants that were expertly tied up to stakes.

This must be what Eden looked like, I thought.

I walked over to the farmhouse porch door and knocked. Rows of little shoes, neatly lined up, were visible through the screen. Nobody was home, so I eventually drove off.

It was years later when I met and grew to love Maureen, the organic farmer with the perfect produce. She was a skilled cultivator of both vegetables and relationships. She invited us to attend church with her whenever we were in town. There we met other salt-of-the-earth people who farmed the land and whose hearts were tilled and open to spiritual seeds planted by God.

And during one dark, difficult life season, our beloved child fled to Maine to spend the entire summer farming with Maureen, who sowed seeds of healing and hope into our loved one's life.

I'll be forever grateful.

Thank You, Lord, for a fresh start, a new year, and the opportunity to show Your love to others over the coming months. Amen.

—Lisa Livezey

GROWING IN FAITH

Think of the people God has brought into your life. What seeds of hope and love did they sow in you?

THE EARTH REMAINS

Generations come and generations go, but the earth remains forever.
—Ecclesiastes 1:4 (NIV)

Winter is a sleepy time in the garden. Snow blankets the earth. Deep within the ground, plants rest dormant, waiting for the return of the sun and warmer days so they can blossom again.

We know that in winter the garden is in a period of rest. We have come to accept this as the natural order of things. I am surprised then, that we refuse to accept periods of dormancy in our own lives.

The book of Ecclesiastes is a wonderful reflection on the seasons of life. The Biblical poet knows that our lives have ups and downs, seasons of new birth and springs and of death and winters. Things change, generations come and go, but the earth is a constant. My backyard garden was a wild patch of earth before my house was built, and when I am gone, this patch of earth will remain.

Winter in the garden is a reminder of death. But as people of faith, we know that death is not the final word. The dormant garden is doing the good work of waiting and preparing for spring. It is a promise of hope for things to come. The days will grow longer, the temperatures will rise, the snow will melt, and again life will spring forth from the earth.

We will come and we will go, but always the earth will follow this blessed cycle of life.

God, let me trust You when life feels sleepy and dormant, knowing that You will help me blossom again. Amen.
—Heather Jepsen

GROWING IN FAITH

Today reflect on the cyclical nature of the seasons and on the cycles in your own life.

WORSHIP IN THE GARDEN

Those who are planted in the house of the Lord *shall flourish in the courts of our God.* —Psalm 92:13 (NKJV)

Attending church on Sundays is important. God's Word confirms that we should congregate with other believers, pray, and hear the Word. God encourages us to sing praises to Him. But for the other days of the week, there's something about a garden.

I feel closest to God when I'm outside in nature, not confined within the walls of a building. The food we grow nourishes our bodies. Flowers nourish our souls. In a garden, we can create a mosaic of colors that rivals any stained-glass window.

I'm not sure how a person who gardens could deny God's existence. Gardening provides a spiritual connection to God, just as the Garden of Eden did at the beginning. Each time you plant a seed or seedling, you are reaffirming your belief in God and the wonders of nature He created.

What better place to worship than surrounded by His creation? What better time to meditate on His Word? To thank Him for all He has done for you and to beseech help when necessary? To sing praises, even if off-key?

So I go to church on Sundays, when the doors are open, but on other days, I find no better place of worship than the garden.

Father, I feel You near as I surround myself with Your wondrous creation. I praise You.

—Kristy Dewberry

GROWING IN FAITH

As you work in your garden, meditate on His Word as you would in church, through thanksgiving, prayer, and praise.

LIVING WATER

Jesus answered her, "If you knew the gift of God and who it is that asks you for a drink, you would have asked him and he would have given you living water."—John 4:10 (NIV)

When I was in elementary school, I entered the science fair with an experiment in botany. I had learned that sodas were fizzy because of carbon dioxide at about the same time I learned that plants need carbon dioxide for photosynthesis. My curiosity was piqued. Wouldn't it be better, I thought, if we watered our plants with *soda* instead of *water*?

I filled five Styrofoam cups with dirt and planted a single pinto bean in each. After choosing several of the most popular sodas of the time, I labeled each cup with the name of the liquid I'd use to water it: Coke, Pepsi, Dr Pepper, Sprite, and water—the boring control group. After several weeks, I was surprised, and a little disappointed, to find that the plant watered with normal, nonbubbly water was the tallest and healthiest of all.

Recently, the Lord has reminded me of that experiment anytime I'm tempted to turn to God-like substitutes for my spiritual growth instead of spending time with Him. How easily I forget that only Jesus offers living water. Only He can help me grow to my fullest potential. Without Him, I will always be thirsty for more.

Lord, forgive me for all the times I've turned to other things to help me grow instead of making my time with You a priority. Amen.

—Emily E. Ryan

GROWING IN FAITH

Consider setting aside one day a week to drink nothing but water. With each sip, thank the Lord for His gift of living water that springs forth to eternal life.

CELEBRATE BIG!

Rejoice always, pray without ceasing, in everything give thanks; for this is the will of God in Christ Jesus for you.
—1 Thessalonians 5:16–18 (NKJV)

My two-and-a-half-year-old granddaughter, Wren, adores the outdoors, and she especially enjoys helping in the garden. Doing anything with Wren is a hoot, but I truly love seeing the ordinary, everyday things through her appreciative eyes.

One day, as we were looking at the "garden of promise"—my name for the garden before the seeds have sprouted—Wren squealed. I thought maybe she'd seen a friendly garden snake, but it wasn't that kind of squeal. This was one of total joy. My eyes followed hers and then *I* squealed: we had our first burst of green leaves.

The garden of promise was becoming a reality right before our eyes. Wren and I celebrated with a little more shouting, and then she broke out into a little dance. No one was looking, so I joined in. We giggled and danced and celebrated.

Often in life, we overlook small victories. We don't take time to celebrate, and we certainly don't break into a dance of joy. But you know what? We should! Maybe you didn't read through the whole Bible last year, but perhaps you did finish the New Testament and the Book of Proverbs. Yay, you! And maybe you didn't lose 20 pounds, but maybe you now move more and drink more water for your health. Way to go!

Let's not dismiss these little accomplishments; rather, let's celebrate and praise God for both little and big breakthroughs.

Father, help me to take time to celebrate
Your goodness in my life—big or little. Amen.
—Michelle Medlock Adams

GROWING IN FAITH

Today write down three or
four small victories and celebrate them!

EXTRA GRACE REQUIRED

"I am the vine; you are the branches. If you remain in me and I in you, you will bear much fruit; apart from me you can do nothing."—John 15:5 (NIV)

I fumed and I fussed. The silver lace vine I'd planted looked like a scraggly stick rather than the fast-growing perennial the catalog advertisement had promised. The pitiful stub of a plant leaned weakly against the corner of the fence. I'd seen similar vines in other yards. Those appeared lush with clusters of small white flowers. Not mine.

"You're stubborn and uncooperative," I scolded.

When I complained to my friend Elizabeth, a skilled gardener, she chuckled and said my vine needed "EGR."

"What's that?" I asked.

"Extra Grace Required," she explained, then expressed her opinion that some people were also like my vine. Her words gave me pause. I had a sneaking suspicion that I was more like my vine than I cared to admit. I often needed extra grace too. *How many times did I get so involved in church activities that I failed to focus on Jesus? How many times had I gone through the motions and observed the rituals without recognizing the holy presence of the Lord?* He wants us to serve, but we can't bear spiritual fruit without remembering that it is Jesus who enables us to grow. *Was I putting down roots in His Word? Was I productively bearing fruit?*

Today my silver lace vine grows rampantly across the backyard fence. And I am concentrating on growing my faith, patience, love, kindness, and the other fruits of the Spirit too.

Lord, help me to cultivate the fruits of Your Spirit. Amen.

—Shirley Raye Redmond

GROWING IN FAITH

Today consider which areas of your life are bearing fruit. Which need more nurturing?

HOPEFUL ANTICIPATION

"For I know the plans I have for you," declares the Lord, "plans to prosper you and not to harm you, plans to give you hope and a future."
—Jeremiah 29:11 (NIV)

Is it possible for a pessimist to plant a successful garden? I highly doubt it. I'm an optimist by nature, and few things fill me with as much hope as planting my spring garden. Preparing the soil after a cold winter and then planting seeds and seedlings that show little indication of a productive payoff should fill me with healthy skepticism. But instead, gardening reminds me of new life. With each deep turn of the dirt revealing hardy, buried worms, I see the potential for my garden's growth. I become filled with hopeful anticipation. No matter how many horticultural hindrances have peppered my past, I am always certain this season will be the best yet.

Shouldn't that same optimism fill our faith lives? No matter how many mess-ups or mishaps we've made, God constantly reminds us that He has plans for us. Like our gardening mistakes, we might still stumble daily. But His forgiveness and love offer us a new season, a fresh start, every time we ask.

Let's not get so caught up in toiling and tending to the garden of our lives that we forget to sit with the hopeful anticipation that is found in God's perfect plan for us.

God, sometimes I become so focused on my earthly plans that I can't see Your heavenly plans for me. Help me to trust in Your perfect plans. Fill me with hope.
—Tamara Bundy

GROWING IN FAITH

Today write down two or three things that fill you with hope. Thank God for these things.

THE BLESSING OF DIRT

He spreads the snow like wool and scatters the frost like ashes.
—Psalm 147:16 (NIV)

I'm not fond of winter, but despite my dislike of the cold, it's the perfect season to work in my garden. The frigid temperatures harden leaves and stiffen winter weeds, making raking easier. Winter gardening allows me to see things I can't see when the flowers bloom. Knee-deep ash in the burn pile forces me to grab the rake and spread it across the garden.

That's where I find an unexpected blessing. Dirt—and not just any dirt: deeply rich, black dirt. As I toss our clippings into the burn pile throughout the summer months, I rarely consider the wonderful gift that comes about from "yard trash" later in the year. This rich soil renews the ground when it's spread across my flower beds. It warms our hidden bulbs through winter, and its rich nutrients feed the roots of hungry plants. God knew the perfect soil mix for His creation, even before I started a burn pile.

I often compare my spiritual study to digging in the rich dirt of the Word. Unless I dig through the layer of ash, the essential things that feed my soul remain hidden. Only when I spend time exploring His Word do I find His reassurances. I'll probably never fully understand God's love, but getting my hands in the dirt of Scripture is a start.

I'm nourished in the rich blessing of God's Word.

Oh God, teach me. Refine me. Feed me. Grow me in Your Word.
—Cindy K. Sproles

GROWING IN FAITH

Look outside today and notice the dirt in your garden plots. Think about what feeds this soil over the course of the year.

LESSON LEARNED

If any of you lacks wisdom, you should ask God, who gives generously to all without finding fault, and it will be given to you. —James 1:5 (NIV)

My first year planting a garden, I had no idea what I was doing. I scoured the racks at the local nursery and bought seeds—mainly cucumber, green beans, and corn, but also squash, carrots, watermelon, and herbs. I filled row after row until every seed was in the soil. And then I waited, watching the seeds sprout and plants grow.

My beginner garden produced an abundant supply of food for the winter. I harvested and canned green beans, shucked and froze the corn, and ate peas right off the vine.

But I soon discovered a problem—I had too many cucumbers. I canned jar after jar of pickles, and I gave cucumbers away until friends and family began turning them down. Soon I ran out of the energy and desire to harvest them. The cucumbers had beaten me. Guiltily, I let them rot on the vine. I eventually pulled the plants and tilled the soil.

Later, I wondered why I hadn't asked my dad, a gardener extraordinaire, for advice about that seed purchase. He would have helped me buy the right amounts of every seed.

Unfortunately, sometimes I do the same with God. I plan my life as *I* think best. And then when I've messed things up, I try to fix it.

My life runs more smoothly when I turn to God whenever I need to make a decision. *His* wisdom is what I need.

Jesus, You see all, know all, and want the best for us. Thank You for Your love.

—Beth Gormong

GROWING IN FAITH

What decisions are you facing today? Ask for God's guidance.

Gardening is the greatest tonic and therapy a human being can have. Even if you have only a tiny piece of earth, you can create something beautiful…

AUDREY HEPBURN, ACTOR

NEVER HUNGRY

Those who work their land will have abundant food, but those who chase fantasies will have their fill of poverty. —Proverbs 28:19 (NIV)

God blessed me with two green-thumbed grandmothers who taught me to love growing things. Both women could masterfully coax abundant harvests from their small plots of land. Instead of whiling away their hours playing Bingo or shopping, they spent their time planting and watching things grow.

"When you plant a garden," my northern grandma often said, "you don't have to depend on others to feed you." She liked to grow escarole, beans, and root vegetables like carrots and potatoes.

My southern grandmother grew sweet corn, tomatoes, and okra. I can still see her sweating profusely as she blanched quart after quart of vegetables to put into the freezer. When the growing season ended, she'd proudly fling open the door of her Frigidaire to display shelves filled with her bountiful harvest.

After she passed away and our family gathered in her two-bedroom bungalow, someone thought to open her freezer. It was still fully stocked with the fruits of the previous year's labor. An index card held to the door with a Western Auto magnet displayed the verse, included above, about the rewards received by those who "work their land."

Unlike my grandmothers, I don't plant vegetables to feed my family. Still, I want to embrace the work ethic they modeled as they tended their gardens.

Father, whether I feed my family by planting crops or by providing for them another way, help me work wholeheartedly for Your glory. Amen.

—Lori Hatcher

GROWING IN FAITH

Consider today who might be watching your work ethic. Ask yourself what lessons they might be learning.

SEEKING THE SUN

This is the message we have heard from him and declare to you: God is light; in him there is no darkness at all. —1 John 1:5 (NIV)

Watching the seasons change through my trees is only one reason I love my wooded backyard. Seeing each arbor change its dressing gowns from budding buds to crisp green leaves, ending in a cornucopia of colors, is like watching God's grandeur in Technicolor. And the fact that they stand side by side guarding my privacy while offering me glorious shade is an extra blessing.

Unfortunately, my plants don't feel the same way about my trees.

It took me one disappointing growing season to realize my garden bed was positioned to receive light only in the short span of time when the sun peeked between the shade of my house and my beloved trees. My paltry harvest suggested something had to change.

The next year, I tried container gardening so I could move the pots around to get more sunlight. This was exactly what my plants needed.

It's what we all need as well.

Living in the shade seems like the easy choice. Shame and insecurity prompt us to hide. But we are created to thrive in the light of the Lord. Sometimes that requires a more conscious effort on our part to remain in His light, but the end result is always worth it.

Growing tip for the world: do whatever you can to stay in the light of the Son.

God, sometimes I get lost in the darkness and forget to look for Your light. Remind me to seek You first in everything I do.
—Tamara Bundy

GROWING IN FAITH

Where do you feel God's light the most?
What can you do today to feel it shine on you?

HIS ETERNAL GARDEN

"There will be no more death or mourning or crying or pain."
—Revelation 21:4 (NIV)

I just put one of my gardens to bed for the winter. It lines my driveway and is new this year. I'm not accustomed to seeing it lie fallow, devoid of color, seemingly dead. Each time I come and go, I'm startled by the loss all over again, missing what brought me so much joy.

Yet it brings me comfort to know that, come spring, there will be an awakening, one with new opportunities for beauty. My perennials will come back heartier and stronger. I'll also sprinkle in some seeds for annuals to witness the wonder of nature as they grow.

I lost my cousin to breast cancer. We grew up on the same street together and were close friends. Even though it's been fourteen years, it's still startling to think she's gone. I keep expecting to see her at the next family gathering or hear her voice on the other end of the phone. The realization that I won't renews that feeling of loss and absence all over again.

Like my garden, it brings me great comfort to know that a time will come when my cousin and I will see each other again. That new awakening will be filled with a beauty so profound we won't have words to describe it. It will be a glorious occasion with no more loss, no more absence. Firmly and forever rooted in Jesus, we'll experience the splendor and joy of His eternal garden.

Resurrected Christ, wrap my heart in peace, knowing
You'll reunite us all in the end. Amen.
—Claire McGarry

GROWING IN FAITH

Stand before your fallow garden today
and praise Jesus for His promise to resurrect us all.

WEEDS OR WILDFLOWERS?

"Consider the lilies of the field, how they grow: they neither toil nor spin; and yet I say to you that even Solomon in all his glory was not arrayed like one of these."—Matthew 6:28–29 (NKJV)

When I go for a walk in our neighborhood, I head for the nature trail. One of the joys I receive from the trail are the different wildflowers that appear along the path during the various seasons.

I stop to admire their intricate details and lovely colors, taking pictures with my phone. In this natural area, I'm reminded that no human planted them there. Our Creator placed them where He wanted them as He designed the landscape. I imagine Him proudly appointing each flower its place as an artist does a finished work of art.

These flowers were not accidents. They were not afterthoughts. And they were no less important than any other plant or flower in the world. However, when these wildflowers show up in yards or gardens, they are often regarded as weeds, unwanted intruders into a carefully created garden plan.

I wonder who decided which flowers were weeds and which were valued. Surely the Master Gardener thought no less of one than the other.

Sometimes we may judge people as having more value than others, similar to wanted flowers or unwanted weeds. But God sees every single person as valuable, equal to the most beautiful flower.

To Him, we are all precious "lilies of the field."

Lord, thank You for the way You love each of us equally.

—Marilyn Turk

GROWING IN FAITH

Next time you take a walk, look for the beauty in the "weeds" and thank God for the reminder of His love for you.

SEED SAVER

"If you have faith as small as a mustard seed, you can say to this mulberry tree, 'Be uprooted and planted in the sea,' and it will obey you."—Luke 17:6 (NIV)

I save my seeds. I don't keep all of them, just certain seeds from quality flowers and vegetables I want to grow in my gardens. I collect the best seeds, dry them, and store them away until planting time comes. I learned this practice while working summers at a vegetable seed research farm during my college years. It is a rewarding process.

Some vegetables, like corn and green beans, lose germination over time if you hold the seed for too many years. Other seeds can remain viable for years, until they are planted when conditions are suitable for germination. It amazes me how such small seeds have the power within themselves to produce blossoms and fruit, provided they have fertile soil, moisture, and sunlight.

While I plant those seeds in the soil, I anticipate the flowers or edible produce that my honeybees or family will enjoy.

It allows me to recall those who planted or watered seeds of faith in my own life and still others who pulled out the competitive weeds to give my faith a chance to grow.

But it was God whose light provided the increase.

Father God, thank You for sending others to water and tend to my development. May the fruit produced in me yield seeds of faith that I will sow into others as You, oh Lord, grant the increase. Amen.

—Ben Cooper

GROWING IN FAITH

Today hold a seed in your hand and prayerfully consider who or what in your life has been planted by God to help you bear fruit. Thank Him!

MEETING NEEDS

And my God will meet all your needs according to the riches of his glory in Christ Jesus. —Philippians 4:19 (NIV)

Sometimes it feels as though I've spent the majority of my life tending to the needs of someone or something else. As a believer, wife, mom, "Nana," teacher, and homemaker, there's always a need *somewhere* that must be met.

That certainly holds true in my garden.

Every year I'm reminded that my plants have needs I must meet for the best possible results—water, nutrition, light, type of soil, and protection from diseases, weeds, and pests. It's easy to get overwhelmed with meeting all of those needs.

But God never gets overwhelmed by the needs of the world. He's always there, taking care of everyone and meeting their needs. He doesn't slumber or sleep but instead watches over His world. In addition to meeting everyday needs for water, air, food, rest, and shelter, He also meets our spiritual needs for forgiveness, salvation, wisdom, guidance, peace, love, joy, and more.

If I stop to focus on *my* needs, my attention moves from the Lord to the temporal. Yet when I place my focus on God and all that He is, I soon realize that He's all I truly need.

Like the Psalmist, I can say with absolute certainty: "The LORD is my shepherd; I have all that I need" (Psalm 23:1, NLT).

Thank You, Lord, for always providing for me, often in ways I don't even realize. Open my eyes to see Your gracious provision. Amen.

—Cathy Bryant

GROWING IN FAITH

Take a few moments to write down how God has recently met your needs, then thank Him!

SURVIVE OR THRIVE?

Not that I have already attained, or am already perfected; but I press on, that I may lay hold of that for which Christ Jesus has also laid hold of me. —Philippians 3:12 (NKJV)

My husband and I moved into a new neighborhood last year, and, for the first time, we finally had room to plant the ornamental garden we'd been dreaming of since moving back to the Midwest. We couldn't wait; however, we realized we'd have to study what foliage could grow in our heavily shaded backyard.

In one of my Internet searches for shade-friendly flowers, I ran across this passage: "A distinction should be made between the terms *surviving* and *thriving*. Many plants can survive in full shade, but that is not sufficient for the purposes of most gardeners. . . ." The article went on to explain that a plant that is underperforming is simply surviving and should be replaced by plants that will actually thrive in low-light conditions.

Those words jumped off my computer screen. I realized I'd been merely surviving and not thriving of late. I had adopted a survival mentality coming out of a difficult season, too afraid to step outside my comfort zone and into the place where God was leading me. I decided that day to trust Him, allowing Him to transplant me so that I could *thrive* for Him.

I challenge you to do the same.

God, help me to step out of my comfort zone and into Your perfect will for my life. I desire to thrive for You. Amen.
—Michelle Medlock Adams

GROWING IN FAITH

If you feel stuck or like you are "just surviving," do one small thing today to move you toward the land of thriving. Take a walk. Pray with a friend. Or just breathe.

THE RUBBER TREE

We are hard pressed on every side, but not crushed; perplexed, but not in despair; persecuted, but not abandoned; struck down, but not destroyed. —2 Corinthians 4:8–9 (NIV)

I live in a condo, and one day while trotting my trash out to the dumpster, I found an abandoned rubber tree. Some leaves were yellowing, some were missing, and, in general, it looked bad. Someone had obviously decided this plant was too sickly to bother keeping. Something told me to snatch it up, so I lugged it to my front patio.

After giving her a generous watering, pruning her dead leaves, and cleaning her pot, I didn't do anything else. She looked pitiful for a while, and I wondered if she would revive. Eventually, though, she perked up and began to grow. The rubber tree actually grew to a full six feet. I then pruned some branches, unceremoniously sticking one in a fresh pot of soil. After a woeful-looking spell, the transplant perked up and started to sprout new leaves. She's now healthy and growing too.

That's an apt metaphor for my spiritual life. Jesus rescued me out of the dumpster of sin and brought me into His home, the Kingdom of God. He watered me with love and acceptance and cleaned me up, causing me to grow. Periodically, He prunes me and transplants me to a bigger pot. Then after withering for a little while, I rebound, stronger and healthier than ever.

Jesus, thank You for rescuing me and watering me with Your love and grace. Please help me submit to transplanting, knowing You're growing me into the person You designed me to be. Amen.

—Isabella Campolattaro

GROWING IN FAITH

Think of a time you were transplanted and reflect on both the initial struggles and resulting growth.

UNEARTHING HIS POWER

My God is my rock, in whom I take refuge. —Psalm 18:2 (NIV)

I learned that an empty lot in town would be paved over to make a church parking lot, so I organized a dig to rescue the grape hyacinth bulbs that grew there. When I spotted some native rain lilies, the minister gave my husband, James, and me permission to save those too.

Together we dug up six egg-sized bulbs. Only one lily remained. With his shovel, James dug into the dirt around the foliage and—*THUNK!*—hit limestone. He dug some more and hit limestone again. And again.

"The lily's in a rock?" I gasped. *No way! How could a bulb grow inside?*

James kept digging. Then he leveraged the shovel deep under the ground and pushed down. Up came a large boulder. When he suggested breaking the rock open to free the bulb, I thought for a moment.

Don't separate them, Sheryl, a small voice whispered. *Your lily's well protected.*

"Can we take the whole thing?" I asked. James nodded. He lifted the 50-pound rock and loaded it into the car.

At home, he transplanted the six bulbs *and* the boulder in our native plant gardens. Three years later, our rain lily in a rock still thrives. It blooms too—a single six-petaled white flower. Whenever I pass by that entombed lily, I smile. It reminds me that I, too, am solidly protected. Every day and night, I'm safe within the rock of my God.

Dear Lord, keep me strong in the knowledge that
no power on earth can surpass Yours. Amen.
—Sheryl Smith-Rodgers

GROWING IN FAITH

Today designate a stone in your garden that will remind you who's the real rock of your life.

CONTAGIOUS CAUSES

And let us consider how we may spur one another on toward love and good deeds. —Hebrews 10:24 (NIV)

It was a silver lining I never could have anticipated. When the class I was attending to certify as a master naturalist was forced to go virtual, I was disheartened, to say the least. Rather than spending days out in our natural areas, I'd be studying local flora and fauna from behind a screen.

Yet what I could not have foreseen was the beautiful synthesizing that took place between my children's education and my own. Taking my classes right alongside me from home, they developed a growing interest in what I was learning. I wanted my kids to garden not only because it's a wholesome hobby, but also because it's a direct way to obey God's call to steward the earth He's created. Together, we learned about the plants we'd soon be growing as a living corridor for pollinating species. Our sense of purpose grew.

As I follow my curiosity, God fuels certain purposes in my heart. He creates these contagious causes that then inspire others around me. In the same way, He places interests in my children's hearts that quickly compel me to learn more and become involved. He is constantly carrying out His purposes on earth and compelling us alongside one another to walk out His great plans.

Lord, thank You for the unique interest You've placed in my heart.
Turn those interests into actions and compel me to fulfill
Your purposes in a way that inspires those around me.
—Eryn Lynum

GROWING IN FAITH

What is a unique interest God has placed in your heart?
This week, take an action step to pursue it and
invite a friend or family member to join you.

THE THORN IN MY FLESH

For our offenses are many in your sight, and our sins testify against us.
—Isaiah 59:12 (NIV)

I kneel next to my flower garden, eyeing the strings of crabgrass crawling over the retaining wall. It won't matter if I pull its arm-length strands on Monday. By Saturday, they return with a vengeance. Cold weather doesn't affect it either. As my late February jonquils peer above a frostbitten ground, the crabgrass has already begun to wrap the flowers in its death grip. I want the annoying grass *gone*.

Despite my efforts to spray, pull, and pluck, the crabgrass has long, deep-seated tentacles stretching in every direction. Unless I can find the primary root, ridding my yard of this mess is impossible. I stand, rubbing the grass from my knees. Its vines leave deep impressions on my skin.

That's how sin is—embedded deep, leaving imprints. Its roots spread, testifying to my sin, penetrating every crevice of my being. No matter my efforts to rid myself of it, the tiny pieces that break off remain hidden, taking every opportunity to sprout again.

I am grateful for a God who sees every inch of my being. Even when I do my best to pluck out offenses, my sin still lingers. Yet the unconditional love of a gracious Father reaches inside my heart and pulls the roots loose, freeing me of sin's grip.

What I can't do alone, God will do with me, and I can bloom and grow.

Father, dig deep into the soil of my heart
and pull out the buried roots of sin.
—Cindy K. Sproles

GROWING IN FAITH

Today sit in silence with God and ask to see what attitudes, behaviors, or habits need to be rooted out for your growth.

STAY PUT

"If you do not remain in me, you are like a branch that is thrown away and withers."—John 15:6 (NIV)

My friend Thea gave me a purple African violet. I knew the delicate plant required specific watering techniques, soil, and food to keep it alive, which was a lofty goal. After all, my husband had playfully nicknamed me the Plant Assassin.

With a little tender loving care, my African violet thrived, displaying clusters of royal blooms. New leaves sprang up and fanned out. Soon the plant was the size of a dinner plate.

Although it flourished, I worried my violet had outgrown its home. I repotted the plant so it could grow even more. Except it didn't. The leaves wilted and rotted until my prized plant could fit in my palm. It should have remained in the original pot.

Like my African violet, sometimes I need to remain where I am to flourish. Recently retired, I fretted about discovering my new purpose. *Open any door, Jesus, and I'll march right through it.* I considered one opportunity after another but never felt a nudge in any direction. Then my pastor said, "If you're not hearing His voice, then you're right where He wants you. If you weren't, He'd let you know."

How true! If I move when I need to stay put, no matter how worthy the opportunity, my efforts spent outside of Jesus's plans will eventually wither. I may wither too. As my African violet needed to remain in its pot, I need to remain right where Jesus puts me. I need to flourish there.

Jesus, thank You for ordering my steps. Please give me patience when I wait. Amen.
—Karen Sargent

GROWING IN FAITH

Ask God to reveal what He desires for you, right where you are.

Hope is one of the essential tools of the farmer or gardener.

AMY STEWART, AUTHOR

TRUE TRANSFORMATION TAKES TIME

But we all, with unveiled faces, looking as in a mirror at the glory of the Lord, are being transformed into the same image from glory to glory, just as from the Lord, the Spirit. —2 Corinthians 3:18 (NASB)

My ambitions are often much larger than what I can reasonably accomplish. When we bought our current home, the landscaping consisted only of an overgrown holly hedge, an enormous sycamore, a scrawny crape myrtle, and some unidentified tree in the front. The rest of the half-acre lot was covered in weeds, intermingled with occasional sprigs of Bermuda grass.

But in my mind's eye, the yard was so much more. I envisioned a white picket fence, vegetable garden, orchard, and flowers spilling out from every spare inch. Though the gardens I've grown since we moved here have done well and are beautiful, I've yet to fully reach that initial vision.

I sometimes wonder if God is disappointed that the garden of my spiritual life isn't further along by now. After all, He's been working on the soil of my heart, clearing out the weeds and planting the fruits of His Spirit within me, for quite a while. I'm grateful to know that as I cooperate with God's work within me, He is transforming me into the image of His Son. I'm also learning to accept that true transformation takes time.

Father, thank You for seeing the potential in my life, even when I don't. Forgive my impatience with the process of transformation. Amen.

—Cathy Bryant

GROWING IN FAITH

Today express to God that you trust His tender care in transforming you.

CONSIDER THE ANT

Go to the ant, you sluggard; consider its ways and be wise! It has no commander, no overseer or ruler, yet it stores its provisions in summer and gathers its food at harvest. —Proverbs 6:6–8 (NIV)

Drip. Drip. Drip. In an indoor faucet, this an annoyance. But outside, in my flower and garden beds, it's the perfect way to deliver just the right amount of water over time, allowing moisture to soak into the soil and hydrate the roots without unnecessary waste. One drop at a time, plants receive all they need both to survive and to thrive.

The ant, mentioned in the Bible, is like this—seeking out and then carrying one leaf or seed or kernel back to the nest. Trip after trip after trip. Day after day after day. Storing up.

What about my own life? A single contribution to the storage chamber seems like too little to make any difference, but when I am consistent over time, small things become big things.

What if I set aside just one dollar a day to give to a food bank? Gave one smile to a stranger? Sent one email, text, or note to a friend? Memorized one verse per day or week? Prayed for one coworker or neighbor, or prayed about what I read in the news? Over the course of 365 days, how would those little things impact my world?

What would I reap from sowing these acts of faithfulness?

Jesus, help me to be like the ant, faithful in the little things so they can add up to life-giving differences in my life, family, and community.

—Candee Fick

GROWING IN FAITH

Decide on one small thing you can add to your daily routine that will impact your world, then faithfully do it.

WHO ARE YOUR VIPS?

Do nothing out of selfish ambition or vain conceit.
Rather, in humility value others above yourselves.
—Philippians 2:3 (NIV)

My friend Elizabeth has a green thumb. Actually, she has two green thumbs and eight green fingers! Her yard looks as if it could be featured in a magazine. She boasts that her lush deep purple clematis is a VIP—a very important plant. So are her spectacular peony bushes, VIPs all.

"Taking care of plants is good preparation for taking care of people," she once told me. "Always keep in mind that when it comes to your Christian brothers and sisters, all are VIPs."

That's good advice, isn't it? Members of Christ's body should treat one another in a special way, serving one another through good deeds.

Do you recall the incident in the Scriptures that tells how Aaron and Hur helped Moses hold up his weary arms while the Israelites battled Amalek's army? Surely, these two men found their own arms growing weary, too, as they supported Moses, but all three realized that the victory and the well-being of their people depended upon their obedience to God. Aaron and Hur were true brothers of encouragement.

I often find myself recalling Elizabeth's wisdom. Loving one another takes time and patience. It also takes hard work. In a manner of speaking, we may also get our hands dirty as Elizabeth does in her lovely garden.

Let us treat one another as VIPs, serving others as we would serve Him.

Lord, help me to meet the needs of Your people
as You would have me do. Amen.
—Shirley Raye Redmond

GROWING IN FAITH

Offer help or encouragement
to a fellow Christian today.

DEEP IN THE MUCK

"Leave it alone for one more year, and I'll dig around it and fertilize it. If it bears fruit next year, fine! If not, then cut it down."
—Luke 13:8–9 (NIV)

This verse, above, is from one of the parables of Jesus. A vineyard owner spies a nonproducing fig tree in his garden, and he orders the gardener to cut the tree down. The gardener begs for a second chance. He promises to give the tree extra attention by loosening the soil and fertilizing it. If it doesn't produce fruit after that, he will cut it down.

This is one of my favorite parables—it is a metaphor for life. We know that fertilizer in the ancient world wasn't composed of chemicals. No, the fertilizer the gardener referred to was manure.

I won't say that God wills our suffering so that we can grow from it, but the fact of the matter is, when we are deep in the manure of life, we do often grow and flourish. It is in our hardest seasons that our faith takes root and is nourished. Sometimes, we need to have our soil disturbed and to be covered in muck before we can really take hold and produce the good fruit of faith.

God, the good gardener, is with us in these times. When we are growing strong and producing good fruit, God rejoices in our gifts of faith. And when we are deep in the muck and manure of life, God is with us, encouraging us to keep growing.

God, I trust You to accompany me through my suffering.
—Heather Jepsen

GROWING IN FAITH

Are you in a season of blossoms or a season of muck? Spend a few minutes reflecting on how God might be helping you grow now.

OF BOOKS AND ORCHIDS

From him the whole body, joined and held together by every supporting ligament, grows and builds itself up in love, as each part does its work.

—Ephesians 4:16 (NIV)

Growing orchids is hard. Very hard. I've tried everything—even the old weekly ice cube trick. Usually, the plant shrivels and dies. It certainly never blooms again. My friend Sue, however, is the orchid queen and raises them with great success. Even when I follow her advice to the letter, I've not been able to replicate her efforts. When I bitterly lamented my failure recently, Sue looked at me with a half-smile and said, "Yes, but you write books. I can't even write a grocery list. If the whole world grew orchids, there'd be no books."

Her words gave me pause. It's true. We all have gifts with which to serve the Lord and His people. Not just spiritual gifts such as preaching, teaching, and making disciples, but other gifts equally important in the Kingdom. Sue blesses others with her exotic blooms. I bless others with my gift of writing. Everything falls under the Lordship of Jesus—from mechanics, healthcare, and accounting to farming and the arts. We all have a meaningful job in the Kingdom of God.

Will I give up on orchids? No, but now I consider them a temporary and exotic flower arrangement to enjoy while it lasts. It's more important that I blossom for Jesus than the orchid produce blooms for me.

Lord, let my service to You be diligent and wholehearted. Amen.

—Shirley Raye Redmond

GROWING IN FAITH

Make a list of your gifts and talents. Consider which one you can employ more fully for God's Kingdom.

BETTER PLANS

In their hearts humans plan their course, but the Lord establishes their steps. —Proverbs 16:9 (NIV)

I'm a planner.

It's easy for me to envision what I want to accomplish, so I plan accordingly. My need to plan definitely carries over into my gardening practice, though I'll be the first to admit that sometimes those plans fail. On the other hand, sometimes things turn out much better than I've expected, not because of my efforts, but because of God's perfect plan.

Such was the case when I decided to try growing my own winter wheat for making bread and feeding my chickens. The seed came from a bag of old organic wheat I'd bought years before and had never used. I didn't expect much, if anything, to come from planting that old wheat seed.

To my surprise, the wheat came up lush and beautiful. Full heads of grain soon developed. Eventually, the wheat turned golden and rippled in the wind. It was lovely—and useful!

The Lord often surprises me with better-than-expected results, not just in gardening but also in life. So many times I would never dare dream for the blessings He showers on me.

How awesome to think that God has plans for me that far exceed what I plan for myself.

Father, I'm grateful that even when my plans fail, Yours never do.
Thank You for so many better-than-expected blessings
that come through Your perfect plans. Amen.

—Cathy Bryant

GROWING IN FAITH

When faced with a situation that surprises or challenges you, look to God with trust. Ask yourself, "Might God have a better plan for me right now than I have for myself?"

GROWING PAINS

When I was a child, I talked like a child, I thought like a child, I reasoned like a child. When I became a man, I put the ways of childhood behind me. —1 Corinthians 13:11 (NIV)

Impatient for the spring and summer bounty of goodness from my garden, I bought a potted basil plant one cold Midwestern winter. It sat on my windowsill, providing perfectly sweet leaves for more than a month. It seemed to thrive, growing taller in the streaming sunlight.

But soon the leaves started curling; the stems began wilting. I tried watering it more and, when that didn't help, watering it less. But still it was dying.

When my dad came to visit, he turned the pot over, showing me the crammed-together roots that had run out of space to grow. Gently, he separated them, and we repotted the basil in a bigger pot, where it once again thrived.

While humans may not get literally root-bound, we can certainly relate to this problem. When we are not doing well, our first assumption might be that we're lacking something. We pray for more. When that doesn't help, we might consider what's in excess in our lives. We pray for discipline, nourishment, growth.

But oftentimes our struggles are simply because we have outgrown something.

Change can be hard. But before that change can begin, we have to pray to see God's will and discern His wisdom. Prayer is often the first step in helping us to fully grow.

God, please help me see what I have outgrown, what is holding me back from growing closer to You.
—Tamara Bundy

GROWING IN FAITH

Where do you feel stuck? Pray for the wisdom to know what to do to thrive again.

EXPERIENCING THE PRESENCE OF GOD

Draw near to God, and He will draw near to you…
—James 4:8 (NKJV)

"Concentrate," I told myself, as I organized my husband's medications for the week. His severe COPD and other health complications required an array of daily prescriptions. It was important that all the meds were in the appropriate pill-organizer slots. But I was having a hard time with this. It had been an unusually stressful, busy week, and my anxiety levels were high.

And it had been days since I'd spent time in our garden. Since reading about physicians in Scotland and other countries giving "nature prescriptions" to their patients, such as bird-watching and gardening, I had tried to spend time in our garden every day. Planting and tending the flowers and herbs were a refuge from the daily pressures and the world's turmoil. But my garden had become much more than that. It had become a place where I experienced the presence of God; it was the place where I drew near to Him and He drew near to me. I set the pill organizer on the table.

"Ten minutes," I said. "I'll sit in the garden for ten minutes." And as I sat, I saw long fragments of morning sun streaming through red begonia petals. I noticed the mosaic of coral honeysuckle and blue mist flowers tangled together. The leaves on the pecan tree rose and fell with the breeze, and my breath deepened and rose and fell with them.

"Thank You, God," I whispered, feeling peaceful, "for Your presence."

God of all creation, thank You for the great gift of the natural world and all Your miracles alive within it.
—Shelly Niebuhr

GROWING IN FAITH

Allow yourself to look deeply into the natural world today and experience the presence of God.

FRAGRANT OFFERING

And walk in the way of love, just as Christ loved us and gave himself up for us as a fragrant offering and sacrifice to God. —Ephesians 5:2 (NIV)

A friend brought me peonies from her garden. Glorious pink petals bobbed on their stems.

As I placed them in a vase, she said, "You can sniff the light pink ones, but don't smell the magenta one. It smells like garbage."

So of course, I had to test that. Sure enough, the pale flowers were sweet with an aroma like rose water. But the magenta one, though beautiful, reeked.

When the sacrifice of Christ is described as a fragrant offering, those words stir me to look at my own offerings to God. How often do I do the right thing but with a stinky attitude? Or serve someone else while hiding building resentment? Or help with a need and make sure everyone knows how much of a sacrifice I'm making?

Yesterday my daughter sent me a bouquet of dried lavender. The color is deep and rich, and the fragrance fills the house. As I thanked her, I told her that I especially appreciate that these flowers will last for such a long time.

Today my prayer is that any tasks I offer, any songs I sing, any service I provide in following Jesus will not just look good from the outside but will also carry the sweet scent of grace and will be valuable, lasting a long time.

Lord, please let us be motivated by love. Bless our efforts to serve You so they might provide lasting glory to You. Amen.

—Sharon Hinck

GROWING IN FAITH

Smell a favorite scent today. Ask Jesus to help your life be a fragrant offering as His was.

A GROUPING OF THREE

Therefore encourage one another and build each other up, just as in fact you are doing. —1 Thessalonians 5:11 (NIV)

It started with a friendly hello after church each week. I had three small children, and my new friend, Jen, had a young son. Jen then introduced me to Steph, a single mom with a four-year-old daughter. While talking with Jen and Steph one Sunday, I expressed frustration over the plantings surrounding my home, bemoaning the cost of professional landscaping. Their response surprised me: "We'll help you," they said.

And so it began. Jen, Steph, and their children visited weekly. The five kids played together in grand fashion, while we moms gardened nearby. Sometimes I'd be assembling lunch for eight while Jen and Steph, elbow-deep in dirt, removed an unsightly shrub or weeded.

Jen demonstrated using an edger to cut out a garden bed, turning the dirt inward for a crisp border. When mulching, she showed me how the pitchfork was a helpful tool.

Steph brought divided perennials from her parents' yard. She arranged the plants in odd-numbered groupings, and explained the pattern of newly planted perennials. "The first year they sleep, the second year they creep, the third year they leap," Steph said.

Soon orderly and attractive landscaping surrounded my home. Even more amazing were the cultivated friendships, which, unlike perennials, leaped the very first year.

Jen and Steph have since moved away to other states. Yet each spring when I'm outside edging and mulching, I remember their hands-on help and ask God to send a practical blessing their way.

Jesus, thank You for being hands-on in our lives.
—Lisa Livezey

GROWING IN FAITH

Is there an area of your life over which you feel frustrated? Ask the Lord to bring help in His own creative way.

A garden really lives only insofar as it is an expression of faith, the embodiment of a hope and a song of praise.

RUSSELL PAGE, PROFESSIONAL GARDEN DESIGNER

LIFE-GIVING WATER

"Whoever drinks the water I give them will never thirst."
—John 4:14 (NIV)

My northern grandmother was a spunky, five-foot-nuthin' Portuguese immigrant with a flair for the dramatic. On good days, she'd clasp us to her ample bosom and squeeze. On bad days, she'd gesture emphatically and utter words I never found in my Portuguese/English dictionary.

Granny's family survived in "the old country" by planting a garden, raising chickens, and drinking milk from the family cow. When they immigrated to America in 1919, they raised chickens and vegetables on a rocky plot of New England soil.

One of my earliest memories of Granny involves her garden. Because the land had no water supply, three times a week she'd fill six porcelain jugs with water from the house. She'd load them into a rickety wagon and pull them down the block to her garden. One day, I tagged along and watched as she gave each tiny seedling a drink.

Reading Jesus's conversation with the woman at the well reminds me of Granny. That is, I watched Granny water her plants with something that *temporarily* satisfied their thirst, but Jesus offers us the water of eternal life to satisfy our souls *permanently*.

We can find satisfaction for every need we have in Christ. He invites us to drink deeply and never thirst again.

Jesus, thank You for lovingly supplying all I need to thrive. Amen.
—Lori Hatcher

GROWING IN FAITH

Today fill a glass with water. Take a long sip, and imagine you are drinking deeply of water from God.

GROWING FAITH

Consider it pure joy, my brothers and sisters, whenever you face trials of many kinds, because you know that the testing of your faith produces perseverance. —James 1:2–3 (NIV)

It takes a lot of faith to grow a garden.

I started my own vegetable garden from seeds this year, but I had mixed results. Some plants that looked healthy in their pots died soon after transplanting. Others, which looked a little weak, somehow survived and produced a good harvest. Some were damaged and killed by insect infestation. Others thrived, despite the insects. And though most years I harvest a lot of squash and corn, this year neither crop did well.

As a gardener, there's only so much I can do. Yes, I can plant the seeds, water, fertilize, and weed. But only God can make gardens grow and produce a harvest.

It's the same with faith. I'm so grateful God can use anything—the trials of life, other people, His Word, our experiences, and even actions that others intended to harm us—to bring about good and grow our faith.

Heavenly Father, thank You for birthing faith inside me
and then testing that faith to make it grow stronger.
Teach me to trust You more in all areas of my life. Amen.
—Cathy Bryant

GROWING IN FAITH

Pray about a current situation in your life, and then step out in faith, trusting that God can use everything that happens to you to bring about good things.

RESCUE MISSION

The disciples picked up twelve basketfuls of broken pieces that were left over. —Luke 9:17 (NIV)

The house where I grew up is no longer there. A construction crew from a nearby airport demolished it, using the land for a runway project. Weeks later, my aging father asked if I'd go over to the property.

"Could you dig up and replant your mother's trumpet vine?" he asked. "I know she'd like that if she were alive."

"Dad, the house is gone," I reminded him.

Still, I went looking. Kicking around in the dirt, I spied a one-inch root sprig with a few dangling root hairs and carried it home in a wad of damp paper towel.

At that same time, I was fighting discouragement, trying to rescue what felt like demolished pieces of my own life. I was facing financial hardship and praying for a child whom I felt had strayed away from the Lord.

I planted the unknown fragment in a flowerpot and watched nothing happen for months. Amazingly, in April, a three-inch sprout appeared. Excited, I called Dad and gave him the news. That fall, a squirrel dug around in the pot, breaking off the shoot. Like that struggling vine, setbacks stalled my own life's narrative. *Lord, when will things improve for me?*

Then, the following spring, a new sprout appeared. I planted it in a sunny garden spot. Today it thrives, an orange profusion of trumpet-shaped blooms blazing in the sun.

Similarly, I call out to my Heavenly Father: "Thank You, God! I see new growth!"

Dear Lord, my life is Yours. Plant me in Your garden of forgiveness, guidance, and love. Amen.
—Durwood Smith

GROWING IN FAITH

Today reach out to someone who is struggling. Encourage them.

ENJOY THE PROCESS!

Be patient, then, brothers and sisters, until the Lord's coming. See how the farmer waits for the land to yield its valuable crop, patiently waiting for the autumn and spring rains. —James 5:7 (NIV)

When my family and I first started developing our farm, we didn't yet live on the property. My father, brother, and I had to drive an hour from our home to do any work and then drive an hour back.

One morning, after getting up early, traveling, setting up, and working, we were able to get only one board nailed up on our project before lunch. This was very discouraging, to say the least.

But in that moment, I felt God tell me something that has stuck with me ever since. He said, "Enjoy the process."

It's easy to be results-driven when the real gift God gives us in *anything* is the journey, being part of His story. When I slow down, take in the beauty around me, and thank God for a garden task, not only does my whole perspective get infused with joy, but also my work begins to reflect the care required to produce the abundance I sought in the first place.

Lord, help me to wholeheartedly live and invest in every moment of my part in the story you are writing.

—Noah Sanders

GROWING IN FAITH

Is there a task in your life that you wish you could just snap your fingers and have done? Ask God to teach you to enjoy the process and the blessings it offers.

OF FAITH AND FAMILY TREES

"Call to me and I will answer you and tell you great and unsearchable things you do not know." —Jeremiah 33:3 (NIV)

My dad grew up on a farm, studied horticulture, and was a true gardening expert. Consequently, when it was time to test my own green thumb, I assumed the apple wouldn't fall far from the tree.

It didn't take too many failed houseplants before I realized I had a lot to learn. I ended up reading everything I could on gardening—and I asked for advice from my dad every chance I got. With a little effort, my thumb grew a tad greener.

That's a lot like my spiritual life too. Growing up in a faith-filled family, I assumed my faith walk would be easy. But it didn't take long to realize that I had a lot to learn.

If we don't continue growing and learning as Christians, our spiritual lives might shrivel up like poorly watered plants. And we know there is no better teaching manual than the Bible. Reading it daily as well as reading other inspirational books and talking to others whose faith is mature may not guarantee an easy walk, but it certainly increases our chances of maturing spiritually.

And while we are talking, it's a good idea to listen prayerfully. How else will we fully realize that our Father knows best?

God, thank You for the faith-filled people and books You have blessed my life with. Remind me to seek them and Your Word every day. Help me to listen and learn. Amen.

—Tamara Bundy

GROWING IN FAITH

Who in your life helps encourage, support, or challenge you in your spiritual journey? Today reach out to someone like that, just to check in.

FOLLOW THEIR LEAD

Consider the outcome of their way of life and imitate their faith.
—Hebrews 13:7 (NIV)

My seventy-year-old neighbor has been gardening her whole life and does so as if it's second nature. Each spring, she's the first one out in her garden. I always wonder why she's at it so soon, as we can't plant until May. *Why the rush?*

Yet every year, when I finally get around to preparing the soil in my own garden, I scold myself for not getting out there sooner. As I'm cleaning out winter debris in the hot weather, my neighbor is sitting on her deck sipping ice tea. When will I ever learn to follow her lead and do as she does?

I ask myself the same question about the women of faith in my life. I see them deep in prayer, carving out time for Jesus well before they ever have a need. Communing with Him becomes second nature to them. It's woven through their days and into the tapestry of their lives.

I want the same thing for myself and plan to eventually get around to it. Oftentimes, though, it's a crisis event that drives me to Jesus. Each and every time, I scold myself for not having gone to Him sooner.

The difference between this scenario and my garden is that it's never too late with Jesus. He takes me as I am, whenever I show up, even when I show up knee-deep in the debris of turmoil.

Ever-patient Jesus, thank You for welcoming me in, no matter the inconsistency of my prayer or the turmoil I bring. Amen.
—Claire McGarry

GROWING IN FAITH

Identify someone in your life who is a positive role model for you. Write them a thank-you note.

PARCHED LANDS WILL BLOSSOM

The desert and the parched land will be glad; the wilderness will rejoice and blossom. —Isaiah 35:1 (NIV)

So much of gardening is dependent on the whims of nature. Will it rain? How hot will it be? When is the last frost? We do our best to make things grow, but we must work within the parameters of nature. Some seasons are wet and some are dry. And while we can cover up our tender shoots in spring and run our sprinklers in the heat of summer, we cannot control the weather.

We also can't control the seasons in our own faith lives.

When I am not working in my garden, I am ministering to my church. I have seen many seasons of faith come and go. Just as the rain is sometimes abundant and sometimes scarce, so, too, having faith in our God sometimes feels easy and sometimes feels hard. Even in my own life I have felt the seasons of faith ebb and flow.

But, always, God's blessings go beyond what we expect. Suddenly in our driest spells of faith, we can have our most moving encounters with the divine. Isaiah writes that the desert and parched land will blossom. I've seen those random wildflowers spring up when I can't seem to make anything else grow.

So, too, in our faith lives God can bring something out of nothing.

Thank You, God, for raining Your love on me. Amen.

—Heather Jepsen

GROWING IN FAITH

Is one area of your life feeling "parched"? Today try to trust that God is with you in *all* things.

GLORY AWAITS

"But as for you, be strong and do not give up, for your work will be rewarded." —2 Chronicles 15:7 (NIV)

Morning glories, aptly named for their radiant blooms in early morning, remind me of jubilant children grinning up at a beloved parent. Although I fell in love with them decades ago, I discovered they weren't easy to grow.

My first crop of blue beauties popped up voluntarily at the corner of our garage. Elated at this surprise, I counted the blooms each morning, reveling in their simple elegance—until a gardener chopped them at their roots along with some unwanted weeds. *Sigh.*

Several times over the years, I've planted morning glory seeds in sunny spots, always presoaking them a few days beforehand. They've rarely popped up, or they produced a wimpy crop. Nevertheless, I delighted in the few that bloomed. Their colorful faces made me smile.

This spring, I decided to plant several packages in two spots, just to be sure I'd have some flowers. One planting never grew. The second planting produced a few pink and purple babies. But near the end of the summer, I spied treasures. Bright blue flowers as huge as saucers upstaged the others. Showing off their azure ball gowns, they shouted: "I've arrived. Let the party begin!"

The giant cobalt blooms reminded me never to give up, not only in growing flowers but also in prayer.

Keep planting those seeds of faith and trust. Rejoice in every tiny flower. And someday the glory will burst forth.

God of all beauty, strengthen me to keep believing in Your willingness to answer my heartfelt prayers.
—Jeanette Levellie

GROWING IN FAITH

Plant some seeds of a flower you've had a difficult time growing in the past. Pray over them, and determine not to give up hope.

THIRST NO MORE

"Whoever believes in me, as Scripture has said, rivers of living water will flow from within them." —John 7:38 (NIV)

She left her plants in my care. I stood staring at the drooping shamrock plant. I'd done everything my friend Pat asked. I watered the plant and even placed it closer to the window for a bit more warmth. *Why had it wilted?*

My knees grew weak as I sat next to the potting bench and inched my bare feet underneath into a small puddle. It took only a moment to realize the problem. I lifted the pot to find no dish under it. I overlooked the missing dish when I'd watered the shamrock earlier. The water had drained through the pot and onto the decking, giving no refreshment to the thirsty plant. I grabbed a dish, slipped it under, and gave the plant some much needed water. Within minutes, the leaves, which had hung low, began to straighten and lean into the sun. The plant's thirst was quenched.

Then an epiphany hit me: my spiritual needs are much the same. If I go too long without making time for God, my soul quickly wilts from thirst. If I do without His Word, my head hangs low. Jesus offers us living water daily. I can choose to let it slip through my fingers, or I can catch it and drink it. And when I drink, refreshment comes, and I thirst no more.

Oh Lord, hear my prayer. Refresh me with Your living water.
Fill me with Your peace and renew my heart. Amen.
—Cindy K. Sproles

GROWING IN FAITH

Today pour yourself a glass of water and think about the way you can quench your *spiritual* thirst as you slowly drink it.

WAITING ON GOD

Be patient, then, brothers and sisters, until the Lord's coming. See how the farmer waits for the land to yield its valuable crop, patiently waiting for the autumn and spring rains. You too, be patient and stand firm, because the Lord's coming is near. —James 5:7–8 (NIV)

"Hey, Julie, guess what I did this weekend!"

My smile was all the invitation she needed, as my coworker took the break room chair next to me, gushing about the tomatoes she'd planted in her first-ever garden.

As I listened, I wondered how to gently break the news that, in her enthusiasm, she'd planted everything at least a month too early, lulled into a false sense of security by a week of warmer-than-average weather. Because of her inexperience and impatience, she now faced the difficulty of keeping her plants alive until the weather stabilized and our soil warmed a month from now.

Planting too soon is a lesson I've learned the hard way, and it's a tangible reminder that sometimes I do the same with God. I run ahead of Him, thinking I know the plan and not understanding that my racing ahead makes life more difficult than it would be if I had been patient and followed His lead.

Following God's timing requires me to stay in close relationship with Him—by reading my Bible and prayerfully listening to Him. His way, in His timing, is always the best choice. Following His lead leads to peace.

Heavenly Father, help me be sensitive to Your leading rather than racing ahead.

—Julie Fisk

GROWING IN FAITH

Practice pausing to pray before taking action on decisions, setting aside time to still your body, mind, and spirit as you listen for His response.

[Gardeners] love the beauty that abounds there, both planned and found. In return, nature responds in kind to love and care.

JEFF COX, AUTHOR

THINNING AND THRIVING

"The Lord gave and the Lord has taken away; may the name of the Lord be praised."—Job 1:21 (NIV)

After we each say, "Love you," my adult son, Sean, and I end our video call. My emotions yo-yo from glee to gloom. Sean plans to apply to an advanced-degree program. How can I not be thrilled? And yet, if accepted, he'll relocate his family to the opposite coast.

My happiness and my son's are entwined like roots, and I sense a root disturbance lurking. As newlyweds, Sean and his wife lived with us briefly before settling into their own place, still nearby. Baby Leon was born, and I've treasured our togetherness. Might the Lord now thin my family garden, removing them well beyond hugging distance?

As a child, I once planted zinnias from a seed packet that promised an array of happy blossoms. Dad urged me to thin the rows after they became established. Crowding thwarted thriving, he explained. I doubted, but I did it. Oh, it pained me to tug up my beloveds at the roots!

Likewise, watching Sean's family uproot would pain me. Will God see fit to offer their young family, His seedlings, ample new room for growth? If He does, I can be sure it's an act of nurture. Just as my youthful gardening faith was rewarded with a superabundance of yellow, pink, and tangerine zinnias, Sean's relocation may result in his thriving.

I'll pray for God's will. And for courage to endure any root disturbance necessary to deepen my own roots in faith's soil.

Lord, where You edit, I know You'll edify. May Your name be praised even when it hurts. Amen.

—Kit Tosello

GROWING IN FAITH

Identify a plant that would benefit from being divided. Gently separate the roots and offer each new space to thrive.

HOPE BLOOMS

For through the Spirit we eagerly await by faith the righteousness for which we hope. —Galatians 5:5 (NIV)

I grew up in the Arizona desert, reading English mysteries and wondering about the plants their authors described. *What exactly is a crocus?* I couldn't tell the difference between a begonia and a fuchsia. Then I moved to Oregon in the dead of winter. I half froze to death, and the bleak February landscape saddened me. Winter felt long; hope was in short supply.

One day, my neighbor began chatting about the coming gardening season. Instead of mysteries, she read seed catalogs in anticipation of her spring and summer plots. I'd never lived in a place where gardens were so important. *But would warmer days ever come?* I prayed for a sign of spring.

One chilly day, I helped my neighbor weed and prepare a garden bed. Amid ground cover and dandelions, I spotted delicate purple, yellow, and white blooms that resembled miniature tulips.

"Are these weeds?" I wondered aloud.

My friend shook muddy soil from her gloves.

"Haven't you ever seen a crocus?" she asked.

A light went on for me. I told her about my girlhood, reading about such things.

"Crocuses let us know that spring is on the way," she said. "They give me hope that winter won't last forever."

Every year since then, I make a garden. When life feels like a never-ending winter, I watch for the crocuses to pop their heads out of the frozen ground. When I spot one, it's like a message from God. I grab a mug of cocoa, open a seed catalog, and dream of summer's garden.

Father, let me eagerly watch for new life, with hope. Amen.

—Linda S. Clare

GROWING IN FAITH

Walk outside and look for signs of spring.

WHEN THE WIND BLOWS

We also glory in our sufferings, because we know that suffering produces perseverance; perseverance, character; and character, hope. —Romans 5:3–4 (NIV)

Living on the top of a mesa, my husband and I sometimes experience tremendous winds. Our house rattles and shakes, and tumbleweeds blow into our yard. The flowers in our gardens bend with powerful gusts, and the plants take a beating. Worried about the wind destroying my plants, I looked online for advice and found out that wind actually works *magic* for plants. Each time a plant is pushed by the wind, it releases a hormone called auxin, which makes the stem stronger.

Similar to plants, when we endure trials, we also grow stronger. For example, I was discouraged when recently diagnosed with osteoporosis, a weakening of the bones. Ironically, like my plants, if I put more stress on my bones (along with taking supplements and medication), they will get stronger. I'm persevering with weightlifting, hiking, and other weight-bearing activities because I hope for a good outcome—strong bones.

When we face a windstorm in life, whether a medical issue or any trial that tests our faith, perseverance works magic for our souls. It's like the hormone in plants that causes stems to grow stronger. Persevering in trusting God, even in the midst of suffering, will eventually lead to character and hope.

Perhaps I should add walking in the wind to my bone-strengthening routine!

Lord, give me the strength to persevere through the trials I face in this life.

—Jeannie Blackmer

GROWING IN FAITH

How has enduring a trial in your life made you stronger? Write down a few words about this today.

THERE'S SOMETHING ABOUT THAT NAME

At the name of Jesus every knee should bow, of those in heaven, and of those on earth, and of those under the earth. —Philippians 2:10 (NKJV)

When my favorite pink rosebush died last summer, I did some research to find a new plant to replace it. I needed something that would survive the high and dry altitude here in the foothills of the Rockies.

I was surprised to see how many roses are named after special people. Diana, Princess of Wales, has a hybrid tea rose named in her honor. The composer George Frideric Handel has been honored with a climbing rose. There are also roses named after Eleanor Roosevelt, Elizabeth Taylor, Ingrid Bergman, and other people.

I'm named after special people too: my mother, Shirley, and her father, Raymond. It is not surprising that I bear certain features and personality traits from my family members for whom I am named.

I also bear the name "Christian," in honor of my Lord and Savior Jesus Christ. The Bible tells us that believers were first called Christians in the city of Antioch. Throughout the centuries, people have worn that name proudly—it stands for something. But with the name comes certain expectations. Just as gardeners who purchase the Princess Diana rose expect a classic bloom with ivory petals and a mild, sweet fragrance—as advertised—I try to remember that bearing the name Christian comes with expectations too. I frequently do a reality check to make sure I'm representing Him appropriately.

After all, names matter.

Dear Heavenly Father, thank You for calling me by name. Amen.

—Shirley Raye Redmond

GROWING IN FAITH

Consider how you might be more like the One you follow. Do one small thing for Christ's glory today.

NEVER TRULY ALONE

God sets the lonely in families. —Psalm 68:6 (NIV)

"Your project is really coming along!" my neighbor called. "The new raised beds look great."

I set aside my secateurs and gloves and crossed the few steps toward him.

"Thanks," I said. "The project hasn't exactly gone according to plan, but that's gardening, right? It's really just one experiment after another."

He laughed, and we began to compare notes about how each of our gardens was progressing. He shared how he was planning to change the way he prepared his hydrangeas for winter.

My neighbor has spent his life gardening in this area. He grew up nearby and is much more familiar with the growing conditions here than I am. I thought he'd gained most of his gardening knowledge from his family. I was surprised when he said a former neighbor had been the one to educate him on the best ways to grow hydrangeas.

Unexpectedly, I began to feel part of a larger community. Instead of gardening being solely a solitary occupation, tending my garden felt tied to generations of people who have tended these very same gardens, sharing freely what they've learned.

I'm reminded of the feeling of connection I get when I step into old churches, the sense that generations of people have faithfully shown up in this same place to tend their relationship with God.

Thank You, Lord, for reminding me that even when I feel most alone, I am still part of a community of people who have followed You over the generations. Amen.

—Chrystal Westbrook

GROWING IN FAITH

Choose a neighbor or coworker you haven't seen recently and reach out to them to share a moment of fellowship.

CULTIVATING GODLY SOIL

"Others, like seed sown on good soil, hear the word, accept it, and produce a crop—some thirty, some sixty, some a hundred times what was sown."
—Mark 4:20 (NIV)

"You look angry."

Lifting my eyes at my daughter's words, I realized I'd been glaring at the four-by-eight-foot raised bed containing my cucumbers.

"I'm not mad, just perplexed," I said. "My seedlings are languishing, and I'm not sure why."

I grabbed my trowel and started scratching the soil surface, squinting with confusion as I uncovered several small pieces of charred wood. *Ohhhhhh.* Memories flooded back of me dumping fireplace wood ash on this particular garden bed years ago, mistakenly thinking I was helping the soil. While I'd used compost and other helpful amendments on this bed since then, I'd never gotten a soil test to determine whether I needed to do further work. My initial mistake, followed by my lack of diligence to fix the underlying problem, was showing up in unhealthy plants.

I'm not so different from those cucumber seedlings. The parable of the sower in Mark 4 reveals that the Word of God requires fertile, healthy soil so it can take root and produce plentiful fruit. When I feed my soul a junk-food diet of cultural fluff rather than a spiritually rich diet of regular prayer, worship, and scripture, I will be weak and ineffectual and produce a smaller spiritual crop than those who tend to their souls well.

Heavenly Father, nudge me toward healthy, spiritually rich food for my soul rather than tasty, cultural junk food.
—Julie Fisk

GROWING IN FAITH

Spend extra time singing to God, talking to God, and reading the Bible this week as you tend to your spiritual soil.

THE PAIN IN PRUNING

I cry out to God Most High, to God who will fulfill his purpose for me.
—Psalm 57:2 (NLT)

Maybe it's the fact that they are my two favorite colors: lavender and green. Or perhaps it's remembering the sweet smell that wafted through my childhood window each summer night. Whatever the reason, lilac bushes are my favorite.

I remember the first time I watched my dad as he took pruning shears to my beloved lilacs. Sure, the flowers had faded and the season had changed, but I was convinced that he ruined them. But after my protests, dad gently explained that if he didn't remove the part that was dying, we wouldn't get the pretty flowers the next year.

And every spring, I would see he was right when the bountiful buds bloomed, even better than the previous year.

Like those lilac bushes, I know that sometimes parts of my life need pruning as well. And most times I don't like the way it feels when it's happening. At all.

Must I strip away those familiar parts even if they are dying or dead? Do I really have to change like that?

The process of pruning can be painful but not if I remember that God is separating me from the things that prevent me from having a healthy relationship with Him.

Like my lilac bushes, I ultimately find myself far better off when I allow Him to cut away what needs to go. Only then can I truly be ready to bloom to fulfill His purpose for me.

God, please help me to let go and trust You.
—Tamara Bundy

GROWING IN FAITH

What in your life might need pruning? Today take one action that will remove something unneeded or unhealthy from your life.

PESTS NO MORE

In wisdom you made them all; the earth is full of your creatures.
—Psalm 104:24 (NIV)

One of the first plants my husband, James, and I bought for what would become our native plant gardens was a flame acanthus. Year by year, the small shrub grew fuller and taller. From summer into early fall, its orange tube-shaped flowers provided nectar for black-chinned and ruby-throated hummingbirds.

Then one day James pointed out a caterpillar infestation on a branch.

"They're going to damage the acanthus," he warned.

"But they're so cute," I countered. The larvae, half an inch in length and ringed with back spines, had red heads and sky-blue bodies. As they munched away, leaf after leaf disappeared.

"How about I just cut off this stem and toss it across the fence," James said. "I won't kill them."

I sighed, then nodded. Then I did some research and discovered that our acanthus was feeding crimson patch caterpillars. *Future butterflies!* I also learned that the species feeds only on acanthus plants. Likewise, other insects often require their own specific host plants. One well-known example are monarchs and milkweeds.

There are no accidents in God's natural world, I realized.

That was nearly fifteen years ago. Since then, we've planted lots more native plants. Lots more hungry critters have shown up too. Other than fire ants, we've not seen any pests all these years.

Every plant and every creature has a purpose. Together, every day, we glorify God's wondrous wisdom.

Dear Lord, thank You for the gift of insects and all they do for our gardens. Amen.
—Sheryl Smith-Rodgers

GROWING IN FAITH

Research what plants in your growing zone attract pollinators and add one to your garden.

IMAGES FROM HER GARDEN

Therefore encourage one another and build each other up, just as in fact you are doing. —1 Thessalonians 5:11 (NIV)

In my mind, I could smell the sweet fragrance of the gardenia, even though it was just a picture on my computer screen. Dark green, glossy leaves showcased the white, satiny petals of its flower.

A tear trailed down my cheek as I read the email from my friend Marilyn. "I want to share some of God's beauty with you while you can still see," the message began.

I first met Marilyn at a writers' workshop. She was warm and engaging and generously shared her writing tips. During the workshop, we all had an opportunity to pitch a story that we wanted to write. I wanted to write about dealing with the blindness that was slowly overtaking me. I'm not sure why I shared so openly with all those present. I don't normally talk about my health issues.

Shortly after I got home, I received the beautiful gardenia email from Marilyn. A few days later, she sent a picture of pink azaleas. Then she sent crape myrtle, vinca, and hibiscus. I could almost feel the velvety petals of yellow roses in yet another email. I committed each flower from her garden to my memory.

As blindness creeps up on me, I hold these beautiful visions in my mind. But more special than that, I keep the love and care of a friend in my heart.

Lord, thank You for the beauty You create
in our gardens and in our friendships. Amen.
—Pamela Haskin

GROWING IN FAITH

Today bring to mind a friend who is struggling in some way. Take a few minutes to write to that friend and include an image of something beautiful.

GUARD MY HEART

Above all else, guard your heart, for everything you do flows from it.
—Proverbs 4:23 (NIV)

I stared at the ten yards of mulch that had been dumped onto our driveway and wanted to cry. It was piled into a mound so high that my children were already climbing its sides and shouting, "I'm king of the mountain!" when they reached the summit. A shovel, a wheelbarrow, and work gloves were waiting for me, and I knew it was going to be a long weekend.

Every few hours, I would question my husband's claim that the mulch was necessary. My back ached. My fingers were raw. I was covered in layers of sweat and dirt. Surely we could have skipped this step!

But with every wheelbarrow, he reminded me that the mulch was not only necessary but also vital to the survival of our plants and flowers. It was a final layer of protection, guarding our seeds and seedlings and keeping them safe from the elements. Yes, spreading it was hard work, but without the mulch, our efforts would wash away in the first spring storm.

I looked again to my children playing in the dirt. They were so young, so fragile. Much like our tiny sprouts and blossoms. I felt the burden and desire to protect their spiritual growth from future storms. The Lord's command to guard our hearts came to mind. I shoveled another pile of mulch into the wheelbarrow and prayed that the Lord would give me the strength I needed for the daunting task of raising them.

Dear God, please protect and prepare me for future storms. Amen.
—Emily E. Ryan

GROWING IN FAITH

What is one thing you can do today to guard your own heart and the hearts of those in your care?

WHISPERS OF SPRING

"As surely as the sun rises, he will appear; he will come to us like the winter rains, like the spring rains that water the earth."
—Hosea 6:3 (NIV)

Spring arrives early in Colorado. While ice still coats the lakes where I grew up in Wisconsin, the optimistic Colorado sunshine has coaxed wildflowers out from their hibernation beneath the chilled soil. Tender shoots peek shyly from between coniferous juniper bushes. Yet the flowers' debut is not permission to plant; we're not clear of winter or its elements.

These wild perennials boast resilient roots and seasoned stems, well-equipped to withstand a late snowfall. They serve as a promise: it's nearly time to plant. Life is returning to the landscape like the warmth and color of a flush in my children's cheeks after an afternoon playing in the cold.

The tiny, delicate petals of the draba flowers are a reliable first whisper. They go unnoticed by most, but they are an anthem of hope, a bouquet of bounty. At my discovery of them and then of the emerging of the elegantly drooping blooms of the pasque, or Passover, flower, something in my spirit revives. If we could hear the "pop" of shoots valiantly succeeding through the hard soil or the peeling back of petals from tightly wound buds, it would sound like a chorus to a faithful Creator.

The Master Gardener who calls the flowers forth in succession is bringing life to the landscape of my soul, and it's nearly time to carry on His work and express His tender care in the soil of my backyard.

Lord, You are bringing new life to my soul!
I see it in every new bud and bloom.
—Eryn Lynum

GROWING IN FAITH

Take a walk outside today,
thanking God for His creation.

THE POTTER'S CLAY

Yet you, Lord, are our Father. We are the clay, you are the potter; we are all the work of your hand. —Isaiah 64:8 (NIV)

In April, my husband, son, and I went outside as a family to ready the soil for our vegetable garden. My husband used the tiller, while I had the grueling task of removing unwanted tufts of grass and weeds. As we worked, my adventurous toddler played nearby. After crawling on my hands and knees for a while, the contents of my bucket were ready to be tossed into the woods. Upon standing and stretching my aching back, I looked up to see my son sitting with his back toward me covered in red clay soil from head to toe. Abandoning my bucket, I headed toward him.

As I got closer, I looked over his shoulder to see he was molding little people from the red clay. Through my toddler's messy imagination, God reminded me that I am molded in His image. He is the potter who fearfully and wonderfully created me with tender care. However, in the evolution of my life, I become filled with holes and rough areas that have been placed upon me through false beliefs, unkind words from others, and wrongful decisions.

When I surrender unattractive areas of my life to Christ, He reveals Himself as the potter who makes me whole. God reestablishes the image of who He has created me to be.

God is the only one who can take my messiness and perfectly restore me.

God, I am confident that You will restore me. Amen.

—Jessi Creed

GROWING IN FAITH

Place your trust in God's hands to heal all your false beliefs, bad decisions, and emotional wounds.

Gardening is something more than a pastime; it is a religion.

PATIENCE STRONG, POET

GOD MAKES THINGS GROW

So neither the one who plants nor the one who waters is anything, but only God, who makes things grow. —1 Corinthians 3:7 (NIV)

Gardening is a humbling endeavor. We can read gardening books and follow careful directions, but there is nothing we can do to force growth to happen. Some flowers in my yard—daylilies and dahlias—refuse to cooperate; I just can't seem to get these plants to succeed. Other plants in my garden—clematis and phlox—seem to thrive without any effort on my part. All I do is plant the initial offering, and those things just take off on their own.

This is a good reminder that we are nothing without God. God decides which plants I will succeed with and which ones will remain out of my reach. God is also the one who grants all growth in our lives.

In 1 Corinthians, Paul uses gardening as a metaphor for the life of faith within the community. Some of us plant faith in the hearts of others, and some of us water and nourish that faith, but only God brings that faith to maturity and full blossom.

As a pastor, I have had to learn this lesson. I can plant seeds, but there is nothing I can do to make faith grow in the heart of another person. That is out of my hands—just as the ability to grow dahlias seems to be for me.

It is God alone who makes things grow.

God, I thank You for the way You've helped me grow.

—Heather Jepsen

GROWING IN FAITH

Take a look at a houseplant or a plant growing in your garden. Think about what you've done to help it grow and all of the many things God does to keep it thriving.

IN THE GARDEN

So do not fear, for I am with you. —Isaiah 41:10 (NIV)

For years, I've loved the old hymn "In the Garden." When I walk through my own garden each morning, the familiar lyrics "I come to the garden alone, while the dew is still on the roses," resonate with me.

During my daily routine, I survey the garden, discovering what new flowers have bloomed or what trimming or weed pulling I need to do. The morning is quiet except for birds whose songs I try to identify. Peace fills my soul as I enjoy the solitude.

Yet I am *not* alone. As the hymn says, "the voice I hear, falling on my ear/ the Son of God discloses./ And He walks with me, and He talks with me/ and He tells me I am His own." Being outside in nature brings me closer to God, and I feel His presence.

The author of "In the Garden," C. Austin Miles, who penned the lyrics in 1912, had a different garden in mind. Miles was inspired by John 20:1–18, the passage that describes the morning Mary Magdalene went to the tomb where Jesus was buried. She was alone, the first person to go to the tomb after the Crucifixion. And there the risen Jesus met her.

When I learned the origin of the hymn, the words took on new meaning as I envisioned the encounter between Jesus and Mary Magdalene, and I imagined myself in that garden with them.

What a comfort she must have felt to see Him risen, a comfort I still feel today.

Lord, thank You for being with us wherever we are. Amen.

—Marilyn Turk

GROWING IN FAITH

Close your eyes and imagine that you are in a quiet garden. Visualize Jesus walking alongside you.

SEASONAL BEAUTY

For in him all things were created.—Colossians 1:16 (NIV)

Each season is uniquely beautiful. Where I live, winter can bring snow and ice, adding beauty to the landscape. But we're more likely to have fair weather, prompting plants to poke their green heads through the soil. Spring is a season of hope and joy as the garden springs to life. Summer brings bountiful crops. Beauty in the fall comes with a slower pace of life, refreshingly cool temperatures, and colorful foliage.

Beauty is also found in the seasons of life. In spring, I first met Jesus and surrendered my life to Him. Summer was exciting, as I went to college, met and married my husband, and gave birth to our sons. Much of the beauty of this season came as God proved faithful and unchanging in my rapidly changing world. Fall, when we became empty nesters, was a challenging season for me. It was sometimes hard to let the kids go, as they started their adult lives. But this season also held the beauty of spending more time with my husband *and* my Lord.

Now I'm approaching the winter of my life, and I'm excited about the prospects. I know this season will come with its own unique set of challenges, but I also have learned that the Lord will reveal His beauty, especially the day when I see Him face-to-face in glory.

Dear Lord, thank You for the beauty in each season of life. Open my eyes to see Your beauty and the beauty You provide around me. Amen.

—Cathy Bryant

GROWING IN FAITH

What season of life are you in now? Make a list of some of the gifts and challenges of the season you are in today.

SHARING PERENNIALS

For just as each of us has one body with many members, and these members do not all have the same function, so in Christ we, though many, form one body, and each member belongs to all the others.
—Romans 12:4–5 (NIV)

A landscape bed in our backyard had been sparse. Deer and rabbits devoured several of our plantings. But one spring, daisies grew and filled in a huge bare area.

The prior fall, my friend Sue had divided her abundant perennials and shared them with me. By spring, I'd forgotten where I'd planted them and even what flowers would appear. It was a joy to be surprised by them.

While gardening, I also realized my yellow irises had flourished and were crowding out their raised bed. I told Sue that when it was time to divide them, I'd bring some to her. She had plenty of purple irises but no yellow ones.

I'm thrifty, so propagating and sharing perennials makes me happy.

It also provides me with a vivid image of the Body of Christ. Jesus has given us different gifts, roles, and callings. Some of us are daisies and others are yellow irises—or peonies or daylilies or lush ground cover.

As we develop our gifts and share them, others can benefit from qualities or skills they don't possess. In turn, we are blessed by the variety of perspectives and approaches to the walk of faith from others.

Dear Lord, help us recognize the unique gifts You've given us and find ways to share these with others. Amen.
—Sharon Hinck

GROWING IN FAITH

Choose a flower or plant to represent your unique gifts. Take a few minutes to write about this plant and the qualities you share.

PRACTICE PATIENCE

Wait for the LORD; be strong and take heart and wait for the LORD.
—Psalm 27:14 (NIV)

I've never been very patient, especially when it comes to putting out my springtime flowers. The first day it's the least bit warm, I want to head to my local nursery and buy enough flowers and ferns to fill up the back of my SUV.

Just as I'm about to pull out of the garage, my husband will flag me down and say, "It's too early." (How does he always know where I'm headed? It's like he has a superpower. Captain Green Thumb!) You know what else? He's usually right.

Last year, winter had been colder and darker than usual, so when that first sort-of-warm day in April came along, I had flowers on my mind. Just as I turned into Leahy's Greenhouse, I heard my hubby's voice in my head, saying, "It's too early. You'll be sorry." So I resisted the urge and headed home. Four days later, it snowed, and I was so glad I'd practiced patience.

It's not easy to wait, whether we're talking about planting flowers or walking with God. Because we live in an instant-everything world, we expect God to operate on our time schedules. But that's not how He works. If God has put your plans on hold, there's a reason.

Wait in faith and remember this truth: God's perfect timing is always worth the wait.

Heavenly Father, I trust You and Your perfect timing. Help me to practice patience and wait in faith. Amen.
—Michelle Medlock Adams

GROWING IN FAITH

Ever heard the expression "Practice makes perfect"? Well, it's time to practice patience! Start small. For example, practice waiting to buy something you want. Delay your purchase for a few days.

SLOW AND STEADY

It is dangerous to have zeal without knowledge, and the one who acts hastily makes poor choices. —Proverbs 19:2 (NET)

Living in the northern reaches of New York State, where the growing season is unmercifully brief, I was eager to get my garden planted as soon as possible. I managed to do so on a single Saturday. Since I like radishes, I planted a lot of them. Too many, as it turned out. In less than a month, I went from being amazed at how quickly they'd sprouted to being overrun with the things.

We put radishes in salads. We ate them raw. We roasted them. We gave them to neighbors and friends. We offered them to the dog. In the end, most of our radishes went to seed, rendering them inedible. Then nothing more than weeds, I tilled them under.

"Such a waste," I thought, looking at the now barren space in my garden. My anxiety about getting a crop before first frost had caused me to squander the very fruit I'd been eager to eat.

That wasn't the first time my haste had made waste. I easily recalled a number of occasions when I hadn't trusted God to bring the right result. I'd made poor financial decisions, I'd broken relationships, and I'd even made wrong moral choices because I lacked the patience to trust Him.

The following year, I resolved to remedy my error. I planted a few radishes each week in the spring, believing that, as always, God's miracle of growth would happen in His time.

Lord, help me to trust You more. Amen.

—Lawrence W. Wilson

GROWING IN FAITH

Be intentional about slowing down a bit today.
Be willing to wait for God's work to unfold, in His good time.

GARDENING BONDS

Fix these words of mine in your hearts and minds; tie them as symbols on your hands and bind them on your foreheads. Teach them to your children, talking about them when you sit at home and when you walk along the road, when you lie down and when you get up.
—Deuteronomy 11:18–19 (NIV)

"Hey, when you're ready to plant your garden," my sister-in-law said over the phone, "call me first. Jena and Jordyn want to help."

My brain began to whirl. I barely know what I'm doing. How will I teach my nieces, two girls in elementary school, what to do? I then spent some time reading gardening books and websites and deciding who would do which tasks, based on age and ability.

The next Saturday afternoon, I invited Jena and Jordyn over. As soon as their mom parked the car, the girls hopped out and gave me huge hugs.

"Jena, you hold the end of the string while I unravel the ball," I said. Jordyn held tight to the other end of the string, across the garden. "I'll dig a straight line between you two."

After the rows were prepared, Jordyn and I planted green bean seeds. Jena followed us, pushing dirt back over the holes. We planted a few more vegetables after the beans, following the same instructions I'd learned in my research.

That day, my nieces learned how to plant a garden, and I was reminded how important it is to pass knowledge on to the next generation.

God wants me to share my knowledge of Him with my nieces too—and what better place to do that than out in a garden.

Jesus, thank You for the gift of time with younger members of our family. May they grow to love and serve You too.
—Beth Gormong

GROWING IN FAITH

Is there a child in your family or a young Christian you can encourage spiritually today?

MESSAGE OF PEACE

Blessed be the God and Father of our Lord Jesus Christ, the Father of mercies and God of all comfort, who comforts us in all our affliction, so that we may be able to comfort those who are in any affliction, with the comfort with which we ourselves are comforted by God.
—2 Corinthians 1:3–4 (ESV)

I was upset and worried about a family member's health and busied myself with household chores. *Please, God, please let everything turn out all right,* I prayed. I had already vacuumed and done the laundry when I remembered there was work to do out in the garden.

It was overcast outside on that warm spring day, and the weeds were easy to pull. Clearing the area around the border of my garden, my mind traveled to what-ifs, and I found myself talking to God, asking Him to help calm me down.

Then I noticed something under old leaves and thick weeds—a small plastic egg from Easter. Years ago, we hosted a family egg hunt and this egg must have been hidden all this time. I shook it, and although it felt empty, I opened it up. Inside was a weathered paper tattoo of a pink, yellow, and blue peace sign.

Peace, I thought. Peace inside an old Easter egg.

I held the fragile paper in my hands, and it happened: I knew God had heard my every word.

Lord, connecting with You is always the way to peace.
—Sabra Ciancanelli

GROWING IN FAITH

Draw a small peace sign and put it in a place you'll see each day—by the kitchen sink, on the bathroom mirror, or on the back of your cell phone. Let it be a reminder to connect with God and share your cares with Him.

INOCULATED WITH THE HOLY SPIRIT

He was a good man, full of the Holy Spirit and faith, and a great number of people were brought to the Lord. —Acts 11:24 (NIV)

Do you remember learning the term *symbiotic relationship* in science class? That is where two different organisms coexist in a mutually beneficial way. In the plant kingdom, legumes have a symbiotic relationship with a bacterium that benefits clover, alfalfa, peas, and certain beans in their germination and root development. These plants start quicker and grow stronger when the seeds are inoculated with the right rhizobia. This produces nitrogen, an important plant nutrient.

My spiritual growth is a direct result of a symbiotic relationship. I was inoculated by the Holy Spirit. This special relationship helped to jump-start my spiritual growth. God inoculated me with the ability to believe in Him for my personal salvation. I was given new life and became rooted in Him. This includes the benefit of faith, which strengthens me to serve God more each day. The much-needed by-product is a spiritual nitrogen that benefits those who are planted around me. As my faith grows, it provides spiritual nutrients for the people in my circle of influence so that the Holy Spirit can inoculate their seeds of faith in their spiritual gardens.

When we live out our faith, God encourages others, just like nitrogen produced by legumes helps fertilize other plants. It all starts by God's Spirit inoculating us.

Dear Lord, thank You for inoculating me with the Holy Spirit, who enables me to grow for the mutual benefit of serving You. Let my testimony nourish others along their journey to glorify You. Amen.

—Ben Cooper

GROWING IN FAITH

Think about the people you will see today. What is one way you could share something about God's love and faithfulness with them?

A BEAUTIFUL AROMA

For we are to God the pleasing aroma of Christ among those who are being saved and those who are perishing. —2 Corinthians 2:15 (NIV)

I love candle and bath stores. You know, the kinds with all of the scented candles and body lotions? I typically go for the beachy scents over the floral ones, and I especially steer clear of anything with a lilac note, so when my husband planted lilacs around the fence line, I wasn't expecting to love them so much. But not only were the cone-shaped flowers beautiful, but also their fragrance was intoxicating. I found myself working in the screened-in porch even on the warmest days just so I could enjoy the calming, lovely smell. I looked forward to experiencing that amazing aroma every day, and I was sad when the first frost took it away.

You know, the Bible says we are to be that same kind of pleasing, refreshing aroma of Christ to an unsaved world. People should be drawn to us the same way I was attracted to the lilac scent wafting into my screened-in porch.

As we live out our faith and allow His sweet aroma to fill us and surround us, it allows us the opportunity to share our Jesus with a hurting world in need of hope.

Heavenly Father, fill me with Your Spirit that I might be a pleasing aroma of Christ to everyone I encounter, and please give me the boldness to take advantage of every opportunity to share my faith. Amen.

—Michelle Medlock Adams

GROWING IN FAITH

When you enter a room, do love, joy, peace, patience, kindness, goodness, faithfulness, gentleness, and self-control enter with you and create a sweet fragrance? Reflect on that today.

All life's lessons grow in the garden: birth, nurturing, love, heartbreak, success, joy, and so many more.

LEE MAY, JOURNALIST

ARTIST GOD

"Do not be afraid, little flock, for your Father has been pleased to give you the kingdom."—Luke 12:32 (NIV)

I never cease to be amazed by all the wildflowers that grow amidst the rye and other prairie grasses on my property. My husband and I live in the middle of a thirty-one-acre pasture. The yard around our house and barn is really just an acre of pasture that we keep mowed short. In an attempt to foster a lusher lawn, I like to allow time for the grasses in the yard to bloom and go to seed before the first mowing in spring. Sometimes it's hard to wait because it gets all scraggily looking out there.

One thing that always amazes me about God is that He did not have to make flowers beautiful. But He did. I believe He did it for our pleasure—and His own.

I find it so much easier to recognize the hand of God through the wildflowers, especially in the tiniest of white blooms that are smaller than the tip of my little finger. Texas bluebonnets, Indian paintbrush, pale pink poppies, and red clover grow in abundance here.

My favorite flowers are the Virginia spring beauties. Their white petals sport bright, purple veining. When I look at the variety and splendor of the flowers in my yard, I no longer notice the untidy, overgrown grass before that first mow.

I see the hand of God.

Thank You, God, for Your extravagant creativity. Amen.
—Pamela Haskin

GROWING IN FAITH

Go for a walk today, even if it's just in your backyard, and imagine the hand of God painting the tree trunks, coloring the flowers, and lighting up the sky with the sun.

PLANTING HOPE

But those who hope in the Lord will renew their strength.
—Isaiah 40:31 (NIV)

I am a pastor, and because of the additional challenges of serving during the first year of the pandemic, I contemplated leaving the ministry. I prayed and God answered my prayers in a surprising way. During "pastor appreciation month," my church chose to honor me every Sunday. Nothing huge, maybe a mug or some candy. It was their way to say: "We see you, and we love you." It meant so much when I was struggling to maintain my spirits.

The final gift the church gave me was a bucket of tulip bulbs. They know I love to garden, and they hoped I would plant those bulbs and that they would be a sign of hope for me in the year to come. Gardeners know that half of what makes a good garden is hope. That Sunday afternoon, I planted the bulbs in my front flower bed so in the spring everyone would be able to share in their beauty. I knew in my heart that day I wouldn't be leaving the church. God sustained me with hope.

When we are tired and sad, our Lord gives us the hope we need to keep going. My congregation did the work of lifting me up and reminding me to hope in the Lord. In the spring, we can all look at the tulips and know that our hope is not misplaced. The flowers will bloom, and those who hope in the Lord will find their strength renewed.

God, thank You for sending me people who reignite my hope in You. Amen.
—Heather Jepsen

GROWING IN FAITH

Who is someone who has encouraged you?
Call them or write them a note of thanks.

THE LORD'S SWEETNESS

Taste and see that the L*ORD* *is good; blessed is the one who takes refuge in him.* —Psalm 34:8 (NIV)

"You'll like, it, Solomon," I said, holding the leaf up to my son's lips. "I promise!"

He wrinkled his nose and turned his head, refusing to taste the stevia leaf I'd just plucked from our herb garden.

I couldn't blame him, of course. His entire life—in each of his eight years—he had been taught not to eat unidentified things from the earth. Dirt, grass, leaves, flowers—they were all off-limits.

"This plant is different," I insisted and chomped down on one. "See, it's safe."

When he finally accepted the leaf and took a small, tentative bite, I could tell the moment the sweetness found his taste buds. His face melted from confusion to delight.

"It's sweet!" he exclaimed and shoved the rest of it into his mouth.

The moment made me think about my neighbors who resist conversations about Jesus. I know that if they would just "taste and see" for themselves, they would discover that the Lord is not only good but also sweet. I forget, however, that some of them were taught—their whole lives—to avoid anything related to God or His Word, so when I share the goodness of God, their instinct is to reject it.

I must be mindful then to let them see His goodness as *I* experience it every day. Perhaps if they continue to see me delight in the Lord, they will want to "taste and see" for themselves.

Dear Lord, help my life reflect Your goodness every day. Amen.

—Emily E. Ryan

GROWING IN FAITH

How can you share your delight in God's goodness with others?

CONSIDER THE LILIES

"Consider the lilies, how they grow: they neither toil nor spin; and yet I say to you, even Solomon in all his glory was not arrayed like one of these."
—Luke 12:27 (NKJV)

I fell in love with our house at first sight because of the extensive landscaping the previous owner had done. He was a retired fireman and had poured all of his energy into making the backyard perfect.

We purchased the home while the yellow irises were in full bloom. The fish pond was surrounded by pink peonies. Sure, I could keep this yard up, I convinced myself. How hard could it be? Turns out, it's pretty hard, especially with my arthritic knees and thumbs, along with some newly discovered allergies.

Friends advised me to "deadhead such and such," "cut back so-and-so," and "reroot this and that." I worried that I would fail and that I'd taken on more than I could handle. My husband and I both worked full-time and couldn't give the garden the attention that the previous owner had.

Finally, I turned to God for help.

"You created the Garden of Eden, so I know You have a green thumb," I prayed. "Please help."

My worrying was for nothing. Each year, the irises return in all their glory, as do the roses and peonies. Every year brings new surprises as well, such as the purple irises that appeared this spring. I thank our Creator for His help.

Father in Heaven, thank You for reminding me to trust in You when I feel overwhelmed.
—Kristy Dewberry

GROWING IN FAITH

Is there a situation in your life that you worry about even though you have no control over the outcome? Turn it over to the Lord.

THE HAILSTORM

Dear friends, don't be surprised at the fiery trials you are going through, as if something strange were happening to you.
—1 Peter 4:12 (NLT)

If you have gardened for more than a few seasons, you know that some years the garden grows exceptionally well and other years are just more challenging. Well, the spring of 2020 was one of those glorious gardening times for me. My field was a rainbow of well-tended spring crops. Tender lettuces, onions, arugula, turnips, radishes, and other crops created a picture of abundance that I would survey with satisfaction.

But one Sunday morning in April, I woke to a sudden storm outside my window. To my horror, I watched as hail began to fall and pelt the ground. When the storm finally passed, I took a heartbreaking tour of my garden. Most of my beautiful, tender crops had been shredded. But as I grieved the loss, I was reminded that God uses suffering to help me grow. If things always went right, how strong would my faith be?

Sometimes I need to be tested to see if my joy is really based in my relationship with Jesus or in having a pretty garden. That day, as I submitted to Jesus and responded in gratitude, I felt an intimacy with my Creator that was stronger than it had been before.

And you know? Most of that garden grew back and gave us an abundant harvest. God is good.

Lord, help me to enjoy working the land but to be grateful even when things are hard, since I know that it helps me to find my joy in You alone.
—Noah Sanders

GROWING IN FAITH

When you experience suffering, pray and give thanks to God. Then see how He draws near to you.

BEAUTY IN MAY

Do all things without complaining and disputing, that you may become blameless and harmless, children of God without fault in the midst of a crooked and perverse generation, among whom you shine as lights in the world, holding fast the word of life.
—Philippians 2:14–16 (NKJV)

I gripped the dash as Jeff, my biologist brother, maneuvered the ATV down a steep hillside path. April showers had carved deep grooves in the dirt, making this May adventure in the woods even bumpier than usual. On our left and right, we encountered spring pastels—the bluish lavender of wild blue phlox, the pale pink of mountain laurel, and the yellow of a nodding trout lily.

Jeff brought the vehicle to a halt mid-hill and turned off the engine.

"I see a plant called fire pink," he said, climbing out. "The blooms aren't really pink at all—they're one of the most vibrant reds in nature."

A few steps off the path, four bright flowers protruded through a covering of dead leaves. How the fire pink stood out from the other colors of the day! Radiant red among soft hues.

The sight perfectly illustrated my calling as a believer: *live* in the world without conforming to it, *demonstrate* the difference of a God-focused life, *shine* the light of Jesus in the darkness.

Those simple flowers encouraged me to glow a shade of fire pink, with rays that reach the people around me.

Dear God, I want to be fire pink during my season on earth. Through Your words of life, teach me how I can stand out for You.
—Becky Alexander

GROWING IN FAITH

Write these phrases: live in the world without conforming to it; demonstrate the difference of a God-focused life; shine the light of Jesus in the darkness. Evaluate your "color" in each area today.

GARDEN THERAPY

See, I am doing a new thing! Now it springs up; do you not perceive it? I am making a way in the wilderness and streams in the wasteland.
—Isaiah 43:19 (NIV)

Who knew gardening would be a therapeutic activity for my son's sobriety? When my twenty-four-year-old first became sober, his AA sponsor encouraged him to adopt new hobbies. He started gardening, specifically growing hot pepper plants and making outrageously spicy hot sauces. This was perfect for his personality—he's feisty, strong, playful, and intense.

Together we planned a garden, his area for hot peppers and mine for other vegetables. When Colorado was past the frost danger, we planted. I watched him tenderly care for his plants. He fertilized, watered, went to battle against critters eating the flowers buds, and poured his heart into his new hobby.

As I observed my son, I saw how responsibly and compassionately he nurtured and tended to his plants. I saw the same traits when he was dealing with circumstances and other people in his life. Without a doubt God was doing a new thing in him. He was making a way for my son to heal and recover. He was making streams in a desert, not only for my son but also for me. In our gardening, I was discovering a new path of trusting God and seeing the new things He does in our lives.

Dear Father, thank You for the new things you bring to life in me and in those I love.
—Jeannie Blackmer

GROWING IN FAITH

What new things do you discern God is doing in your life? In the lives of people you know? Write down what you see.

TEARS TO JOY

Those who sow with tears will reap with songs of joy.
—Psalm 126:5 (NIV)

One warm spring day, I knew it was the perfect time to plant seeds for my flower garden. Everything was going as planned when a light rain misted the newly planted seeds. According to an old wives' tale, a light rain after planting is an omen for a successful garden. Unfortunately, it turned into a nonstop, torrential downpour for a week. I had the sinking feeling my seeds either drowned or were washed away.

My family was facing its own storm then. My three-year-old son was diagnosed with a very rare condition, and we were dealing with ongoing doctors' appointments, medical therapies, and tests. There were so many days when I thought I was going to drown, just as I imagined those seeds did. I was afraid that what I loved so dearly would be washed away. These circumstances distracted me from the flower garden, and I forgot all about those seeds. That is, until one day when I stepped out onto the deck and found beautiful flowers and a hummingbird enjoying sweet nectar. When a blue butterfly landed nearby, I scooped it on my finger and marveled at its fragile beauty.

That moment foreshadowed a turning point for my son. Shortly after, we received miraculous news. With each medical victory, my family celebrated with dancing, shouts of praise, and singing. In the process, I learned to trust in God's faithfulness by placing my fears at His feet as He wiped away my tears and replaced them with songs of joy.

Father, thank You for always being with me! Amen.
—Jessi Creed

GROWING IN FAITH

Take a short walk outdoors today. Tell God that you trust Him, even in difficult seasons.

GOD MOMENTS IN THE GARDEN

Now to him who is able to do immeasurably more than all we ask or imagine, according to his power that is at work within us.
—Ephesians 3:20 (NIV)

As a Texas gal, I adore bluebonnets. Our state flower is by far my favorite symbol of this vast and diverse place. When we moved back to Texas three years ago, the very first plant I bought was a Texas bluebonnet. I had tried growing them in the other places we've lived but without success. So I took solace in that one small plant, certain I would have to buy another one the following year.

Boy, was I wrong. The next spring, I had a handful of bluebonnets coming up in my flower bed. And this year, they surpassed the previous two years by spreading across the entire flower bed and spilling through the picket fence until they reached the curb.

In truth, my abundance of bluebonnets proves how good, gracious, and generous our God is. All His gifts are good and perfect. Nothing is impossible for Him. He regularly showers us with blessings, and His work is often immeasurably more abundant than we could ever ask for or imagine.

This kind of "God moment" in gardening keeps me grateful to the Lord for His super-abundant blessings.

I can't wait to see what He does next to show how good He is.

Lord God, how awesome and wonderful You are. Open my eyes to see Your goodness. May it lead me to gratefulness and praise. Let me quickly give You the credit and glory when others admire Your work in my garden. Amen.

—Cathy Bryant

GROWING IN FAITH

Look for God's blessings outside in nature, and allow them to move you to gratitude and praise.

GOODBYE TO THE DAISIES

For like grass they will soon wither, like green plants they will soon die away. —Psalm 37:2 (NIV)

Oxeye daisies have always been one of my favorite gifts from God. Where I live, they grow in profusion in roadside ditches and fields throughout the month of May. As a child, I gathered fistfuls of daisies and sat cross-legged on the grass, plucking the delicate white petals, one by one.

"He loves me, he loves me not," I'd whisper, hoping that when nothing remained except the stem and yellow center, I'd have proof of a boyfriend's affection.

I gave up that silly game when I became an adult, but I still adored daisies. In spring, I kept a pair of scissors and a coffee can filled with water in my car so if I happened upon a patch of wild daisies I could stop and cut a bouquet for my table. Eventually, I realized it would be easier to grow my own daisies than to forage for them.

So late one autumn, I dug up a sunny patch of ground, scattered seeds, and kept them watered. The daisies that appeared in my flower bed the next spring were just as lovely as those that grew wild. But when summer's heat became intense, they drooped and withered. It was time to weed-whack them to the ground.

Before I began, I noticed a single perfect daisy smiling up at me. I picked it and sank down cross-legged onto the grass, grateful that every May—without fail—God sends me daisies. And no matter how the petal-plucking comes out, I know He loves me.

Father, thank You for the simple wonder of daisies... and Your love.

—Jennie Ivey

GROWING IN FAITH

Write down one simple blessing God has given you.

No one can make a garden by buying a few packets of seeds or doing an afternoon's weeding. You must love it, and then your love will be repaid a thousandfold...

MARGERY FISH, GARDEN WRITER

TOUGHER THAN THEY LOOK

Blessed is the one who perseveres under trial because, having stood the test, that person will receive the crown of life that the Lord has promised to those who love him. —James 1:12 (NIV)

The lilies of the valley in my front flower beds took a beating from a construction project. Their tender pips were trampled, raked, smashed, and then smothered with landscape gravel. They were then missing in action, and I presumed them dead.

If a person can grieve over the loss of a flower, that's what I did. Grieve. For almost forty years, those persistent, artistic, delicate flowers had represented spring to me. They represented unmatched beauty written about in poetry and Scripture and God's creative genius.

I stared at the barren, graveled lily grave, once so lush with bright green leaves and tiny stems of graduated, frilled bells. My heart felt heavy. If those then-absent flowers could have spoken to me, they would have said, "Honey, you just wait!"

Yes, they rebounded. It took a long time, but my front flower beds once again burst with delicate white bells whose fragrance drifts through the windows and whose pips find their way, without my intervention, beyond their original beds.

Today I'm more aware than ever that what seems dead isn't always permanently lost. Lost dreams, broken relationships, crushed and barren hopes. Not necessarily dead. Perhaps just deep underground, fighting their way back up to the top to bloom again.

Thank You, Lord, for reminding me that with Your help, even what seems dead or gone may be resurrected by Your power. Amen.
—Cynthia Ruchti

GROWING IN FAITH

If you are mourning the loss of a relationship or the death of a dream, surrender it to God today and watch for signs of new life.

THE TIGER MOTH

And we all, who with unveiled faces contemplate the Lord's glory, are being transformed into his image with ever-increasing glory, which comes from the Lord, who is the Spirit. —2 Corinthians 3:18 (NIV)

Early spring, I began the long process of planning my garden. I was distracted by worries, including my son starting at a new school and my own new responsibilities at work. Change has never been easy for me.

Moving aside a walking board, I found about a dozen woolly bears all curled up, seemingly frozen. I love woolly bears—those furry black and brown caterpillars. Some people believe that the color of their coats can predict the severity of the winter: mostly brown means a mild winter and thick black bands mean a snowy, frigid one. I carefully placed the board back and hoped I hadn't disturbed their hibernation.

Weeks later, I was struggling with answering an email. I had gotten up to clear my head and decided to go outside to the garden. I spotted an odd, hairy pod hanging from last year's grapevine. On closer inspection, I realized it was an empty cocoon, and on a nearby branch, a stone's throw from where the woolly bear made its metamorphosis, an Isabella tiger moth waited.

Although the moth was completely motionless, I felt my spirit soar at the miracle of its journey from a frozen caterpillar to a glorious, winged creature.

It served as a beautiful reminder to trust God through all the changes in life.

Lord, maker of butterflies and beautiful things, thank
You for the magnificent plans You have for me.
—Sabra Ciancanelli

GROWING IN FAITH

Reflect on a positive change you can make in your life that will glorify God.

LIVE TO GIVE

One person gives freely, yet gains even more; another withholds unduly, but comes to poverty. —Proverbs 11:24 (NIV)

I love hummingbirds, so when we moved into our new home, my husband and I decided to plant a garden that would attract them. Thankfully, he likes hummingbirds as much as I do and had already begun researching the kinds of "hummingbird magnets" we could place around our pool.

We then learned hummingbirds are partial to the color red, so we put out red trumpets, cardinal flowers, Texas sage, and Mexican cigar plants. In time, the flowers bloomed, and the hummingbirds arrived. You would not believe how many showed up at our house—at least initially.

After a few days, I noticed fewer hummingbirds flitting about, and soon I knew why. We had a hostile hummingbird—a bully bird—guarding the entire pool area. This aggressive little guy patrolled the hummingbird plants all day but hardly ever took a drink because he was too busy protecting his space. His stinginess stood in the way of his nourishment.

Truth is, we all have a little hostile hummingbird in us. We can become so protective of what we have that we fail to even enjoy it.

But being stingy is never God's way. We are meant to live generously, recognizing that everything we have is from God. Let's not be like the hummingbird and keep the blessings we've found to ourselves. Let's live to give. Our Heavenly Father has more than enough to go around.

God, grow a generous heart in me. Thank You for all that I have. Amen.
—Michelle Medlock Adams

GROWING IN FAITH

Look for ways to bless someone today.
For example, pay for the person's order behind
you in the drive-through line.

DIGGING COMMUNITY

And the LORD *God said, "It is not good that man should be alone..."*
—Genesis 2:18 (NKJV)

Around the corner from my house, a community garden's raised beds abound with colorful plant life. Today several people are bent over various rows, digging and weeding. A woman in a wide-brimmed hat lifts her focused face. But when another gardener says something to her, the music of her laughter drifts through the wire fence and across the road to me. Two more gardeners engage in leisurely conversation. Exchanging gardening tips? Something more personal?

Today I'm out walking because I've become uninspired in my own work, a writing project. I feel stuck, and I'm praying a solution falls from the sky. But watching these gardeners share resources and camaraderie, I feel something else as well. A pang of envy.

Maybe this is my solution—community. Maybe my river of inspiration has dried up because I'm lonely, and I could use the kind of watering that happens only in the company of others.

I'm reminded of my favorite gardening memory—of planting and tending side by side with my father. And my favorite day of the month is when my writer's group meets. I always come away rejuvenated. We call ourselves the Daring Sisters. Maybe today being daring means reaching out to one of those writerly sisters and exchanging ideas over a mug of chai.

After all, God didn't design His children or gardeners to go it alone.

Lord, give me wisdom to know when I need advice, encouragement, or companionship. Embolden me to step into community.
—Kit Tosello

GROWING IN FAITH

Whose companionship would most edify you today? Or, if you're struggling with a problem, who might you turn to for advice? Schedule a meetup, in person if possible.

FLOWER BED WISDOM

For you have been born again, not of perishable seed, but of imperishable, through the living and enduring word of God. —1 Peter 1:23 (NIV)

Each summer I drive by our former home on Walnut Street to admire the colorful array of flowers along the fence—from bachelor buttons and cosmos to a rainbow assortment of zinnias. My son Jordan planted those flowers when he was a boy. He'd gone to the hardware store with my husband, Bill, and spotted rolls of preseeded flower mats. He begged his dad to buy them to plant along the fence that separated our house from the neighbor's. Jordan promised to do all the work. My husband bought the mats, and together they read the growing instructions, tilled the soil, and planted the preseeded flower mats. Bill cautioned him about invasive weeds and the need for sufficient watering.

As Jordan waited eagerly for the first sprouts, Bill said, "Remember, when it comes to gardening, there's the part you do and the part God does."

Looking back, I realize that my husband's advice applies to our spiritual growth too: there's the part we do and the part God does. Without regular worship, Bible study, and prayer, we cannot expect to blossom or become more Christlike.

Jordan's hard work paid off. A kaleidoscope of color brightened our yard by summer's end, and it became a favorite backdrop for family photos. It brightens Walnut Street even now. Jordan had done his part and God had done His.

Lord, help me to bloom where I'm planted, growing more like Christ each day. Amen.

—Shirley Raye Redmond

GROWING IN FAITH

Consider what you can do today to grow closer to God and make a commitment to do so.

HARDER THAN IT HAS TO BE

But the seed falling on good soil refers to someone who hears the word and understands it...yielding a hundred, sixty or thirty times what was sown. —Matthew 13:23 (NIV)

The soil in my garden's raised beds had become compacted from years of amending and fertilizing. One spring, when my husband was unable to turn over the soil with his mighty pitchfork, I took my handheld spade and dug down in winter-hardened soil only as far as the blade would reach. I crammed my tomato plants into the small, peat-pot-sized holes I'd made. The tomatoes grew; they're stubborn that way. But the plants' roots had to fight so hard to burst through the hard soil and dive for nutrients and stability that the crop was much less than I'd hoped.

Yes, another gardening failure served as a classroom for my soul.

Why do I make it harder than it needs to be for good things to take root in me? What if I'd waited and turned the soil over properly? What kind of crop might have grown then? What might happen if I spend more time in God's Word today, more time listening and letting my heart soften to what He wants to plant there?

It might take an investment today to dig deeper, but the bountiful harvest from that extra time and effort will be worth it.

God, work the "soil" of my soul in preparation for roots of peace, patience, kindness, gentleness. And remind me in Your Word of the folly of not letting You dig deep. Amen.

—Cynthia Ruchti

GROWING IN FAITH

Where do you need to grow? Forgiveness? Study of God's Word? Understanding His love for you? Don't be afraid to dig deep to grow deeply in Christ.

SEEDS THAT LAST

God will never be mocked! For what you plant will always be the very thing you harvest. —Galatians 6:7 (TPT)

I'm a sucker for seeds. Those spin racks that display every kind of vegetable and flower seed zap me like a magnet whenever I enter a farm and garden store. My cry every spring is: "I want everything I see!"

This spring, I tried something different. I bought a huge package of wildflower seeds already mixed with soil. All I did was soften the earth in the flower bed, sprinkle the seed mix, and cover it with an inch of soil. In a couple weeks, we had a circus of color underneath our living room window. Feathery-leaved cosmos in pale pastels, smiling zinnias of fuchsia and orange, even a few sky-blue bachelor buttons. They lasted into the fall months, dancing in defiance at the stinging breezes.

The verse above used to make me nervous. In the course of my life—especially when I was young and immature—I planted some ugly seeds of rage, manipulation, and unkindness. What would the flower bed of my future look like? Yikes!

But then I remembered Jesus's promise to cleanse me of every sin I confessed. His sweet Spirit also reminded me of the many loving, unselfish seeds I'd planted. God is *for* me, not against me. He's the Master Gardener who plucks out every rotten seed I've planted. And then He teaches me how to plant seeds of love.

Lord, thank You for forgiving me when I sin and offering me daily opportunities to redo my life. Amen.

—Jeanette Levellie

GROWING IN FAITH

Close your eyes and envision yourself planting seeds of kindness, understanding, and self-control. Now imagine the flower bed of your future brimming with gorgeous blooms.

WATCH THE WILDFLOWERS GROW

Consider how the wild flowers grow. They do not labor or spin.
—Luke 12:27 (NIV)

Recently, I launched an Instagram account. I wanted to post uplifting devotions on a platform that often leaves people discouraged. I hired a graphic designer to create compelling images, and I purchased ads to boost views of my devotions. Week after week, I posted a new devotion with a professional image and paid for the ad. I checked the analytics several times a day, but my readership did not grow as much as I'd hoped it would. I was spinning to force my Instagram followers to increase, but they weren't. My laboring left me discouraged.

At the same time, my son and I spread two million wildflower seeds on our property. We mixed them with sand and, just before a wet spring snowstorm, we tossed the seeds on the ground. A few months later, the wildflowers bloomed abundantly. We had sprinklings of spectacular flowers bursting everywhere.

As I admired the abundance of the wildflowers, I was reminded not to rely on my own efforts to achieve what I desire. God creates and cares for the wildflowers. *They* do not labor and spin, and they bloom spectacularly. How much more will He do for me?

I decided to let that Instagram account go. I'm still writing devotions, scattering those seeds, and I'm trusting He'll get them to the people who need them the most.

Father, thank You for the wildflowers in my yard and
for reminding me that You are in control.
—Jeannie Blackmer

GROWING IN FAITH

Toss some wildflower seeds on the ground or make a motion as though you are scattering seeds. As you do, imagine letting go of something you're laboring over and release control to God.

FAITHFULLY CONSTANT

So we are Christ's ambassadors; God is making his appeal through us. We speak for Christ when we plead, "Come back to God!"
—2 Corinthians 5:20 (NLT)

For most of the year when I step into my garden, I'm greeted by my cheery and colorful zinnias. These flowers spring up from the previous year's seeds. Unless they're where I plan to grow something else, I let them stay wherever they choose to grow.

It's always so encouraging and uplifting to see their smiling faces and happy demeanor. I can't help but smile in return at their friendly greeting.

I think of them as goodwill ambassadors, doing their job, no matter what. Excessive heat, an overabundance of rain, no rain at all—they remain the same cheery flowers that bid me good morning and gladden my heart. Nothing seems to affect their mood.

Just like zinnias, we're ambassadors too. We are ambassadors for Christ.

I want to be like those zinnias! No matter what's going on around me, whether sorrow or sickness or something threatening to distract me from my task, I want to reflect God's light, love, hope, and encouragement to all I meet.

Lord Jesus, remind me daily that I'm on a mission for You as Your ambassador. Amen.
—Cathy Bryant

GROWING IN FAITH

On a card or sticky note, write down the verse above and place it where you'll see it as a reminder every time you leave your home. *You* are Christ's ambassador!

WAITING WELL

Be still before the LORD and wait patiently for him.
—Psalm 37:7 (NIV)

The practice of gardening sets our internal clocks and calendars to a new cadence. Spring becomes our axis. The weeks that precede the ground's thawing are brimming with anticipation. As a gardener, I find this waiting can feel, at times, excruciatingly long. After a drawn-out winter, I ache to watch life press through the soil. My fingers feel itchy, ready, eager to dig into the dirt... but I have to wait. All winter, ideas and plans and hopes for our pollinator garden have danced in my head, and it's nearly time to put them to work. Once my mind settles on a plan, I want to immediately begin executing it.

But God has a purpose behind these seasons of waiting. After God called the Apostle Paul into ministry, Paul didn't go right to work. Instead, in Galatians 1, we see him spending three entire years in preparation. His waiting was not idle, and mine doesn't have to be either. Just like Paul, God has much to teach me before I can see a plan through to fruition.

Good plants emerge from well-prepared ground. Water, oxygen, organic materials, and nutrients create a system intent on nourishing the plants I'm so eager to sow in the garden. In the same way, God is preparing my heart. He's working all things toward my good and His glory.

Lord, I recognize Your active hand in this season of waiting. Help me to see the many ways You are growing and preparing me for all You have in store.
—Eryn Lynum

GROWING IN FAITH

What is something you are waiting for today?
Write it down, along with two or three ways you sense
God growing and teaching you in this time.

LASTING BENEFITS

Being confident of this, that he who began a good work in you will carry it on to completion until the day of Christ Jesus. —Philippians 1:6 (NIV)

Asparagus is a vegetable that people either love or hate. For some, it is an acquired taste. I enjoy growing and eating it. When I see the first green spears poking through the ground, I get excited, imagining it on my dinner plate.

Almost every vegetable I plant is an annual, meaning I must plant it every year. Asparagus, however, is a perennial, and a well-maintained asparagus bed can last up to forty years! I planted crowns instead of seeds and they have been in the ground for thirty-two years. I harvest the asparagus during April and May each year and then let it mature and go to seed. My management style is successful in keeping the bed viable. This results in an asparagus patch that has lasted for decades.

My asparagus patch reminds me of how I came into a relationship with the Lord at the age of twelve. A bed was prepared in the garden of my soul to receive the seed of faith that grew to produce fruit for decades. Each year, God tends to my needs and fruit comes in due season. That seed that has been planted provides lasting harvest. He awards believers with the crown of life.

Heavenly Father, thank You for establishing the seed of faith in me. Help me to grow and produce lasting benefits for decades. Amen.

—Ben Cooper

GROWING IN FAITH

Think about when you first came to know the Lord. Thank Him today for seeing you through the years, lovingly maintaining the garden of your soul.

HOLDING FAST

"Love the Lord your God, walk in all his ways, obey his commands, hold firmly to him, and serve him with all your heart and all your soul."
—Joshua 22:5 (NLT)

Nothing in the garden "holds fast" like a clematis vine. When we moved to our house six years ago, I planted clematis next to an old swing trellis in the backyard. My plants were from a discount store, and when I put them in the ground, they were literally nothing more than a stick with a few roots. Because I watered and tended them, they are now much taller than I am and have completely taken over the trellis.

Clematis is interesting because it won't hold on to just anything. My vines love clinging to a metal trellis, other plants, or even a piece of string. But they hate the treated wood that is near them. It is fascinating to me that the vine can get so large but also avoid the main structure it is planted around.

In the verse above from Joshua, the Israelites have finally made it into the Promised Land and Joshua is giving the people advice for the years ahead. If they are going to be successful, they need to hold fast to God. There will be many things to distract them, but if they can hold fast to the Lord, they will grow strong and true.

The way that the clematis chooses what it will cling to, and wraps around tight when it finds it, is such a wonderful reminder to me to cling to my God.

God, I cling to Your love.
—Heather Jepsen

GROWING IN FAITH

Look outside at a tree today. Imagine your own spiritual roots holding fast to the Lord. Thank Him for His protection.

God Almighty planted a garden. And indeed, it is the purest of human pleasures.

SIR FRANCIS BACON, PHILOSOPHER

TENDING A GARDEN, TENDING YOUR HEART

Carry each other's burdens, and in this way you will fulfill the law of Christ. —Galatians 6:2 (NIV)

When I heard the table saw and then noticed my husband and twelve-year-old son, Isaiah, hunkered down over long slats of wood on the driveway, I was curious. Were they organizing the garage? We'd recently moved out of our beloved Victorian house, and everything was out of place at our new home.

I went back into the kitchen to place familiar bowls on unfamiliar shelves, but soon I heard the *crack-crack-crack* of a hammer. I followed the sound. When I stood over my young son, he looked up and squinted in the sunshine.

"You're going to love them, Mom," he said.

"Shelves?" I asked.

Isaiah beamed. "No, garden boxes. You've always wanted a garden."

It was true. The yard of our Victorian had held lovely, old maples that shaded everything. But our new yard was empty. Sunshine splayed.

I stood for a moment and glanced over at the garage. Boxes were stacked like stone walls. There was much to do. Yet it was late spring and there was still time to plant a garden.

Isaiah went back to hammering. His long, blond bangs fell forward. He knew how hard the move had been for me. He also knew that gardens are for growing new life, places where the Lord's provision is apparent.

My soul swelled. "Thank you," I said.

My boy and his daddy nodded and went back to work.

I looked forward to tending the garden these boxes would hold and was grateful for how these men tended to my heart.

Lord, help me to see the burdens of others
and to help lighten the load. Amen.
—Shawnelle Eliasen

GROWING IN FAITH

What can you do today to ease someone's grief or pain?

SHARING FAITH AND DAFFODILS

For I am not ashamed of the gospel, because it is the power of God that brings salvation to everyone who believes. —Romans 1:16 (NIV)

One of the sweetest legacies my southern grandmother left behind wasn't mentioned in her will or cataloged with the contents of her estate. It was buried in her backyard. Unlike the legendary tales of long-lost treasure, Granny's golden gift didn't send kids to college or make anyone rich, but it has prompted a lot of smiles.

Shortly after her funeral, my mom called me.

"Can you meet me at Granny's house?" she asked. "I need your help."

I assumed we'd work inside inventorying goods for the upcoming estate sale. Instead, she met me in the yard and handed me a shovel.

"We have to dig up the daffodil bulbs," she said. "We can't just leave them here."

I agreed. Granny's daffodil garden in the spring was breathtaking.

We must have dug up 200 bulbs from around her dogwood tree. We divided and planted them in our yards, where they bloomed and multiplied. When we moved, I dug up Granny's bulbs and took them with me. I planted some and shared the rest with friends. The next spring, one of those friends sent me a picture of "Granny's daffodils" blooming profusely in her backyard.

I've come to realize that faith is a lot like daffodil bulbs. Not only is it breathtakingly beautiful, but it is also meant to be shared. It brings joy to the one who gives it away and joy to the One who receives it.

Lord, may I be as eager to share my faith as I am to share other joy-filled blessings You provide. Amen.

—Lori Hatcher

GROWING IN FAITH

Ask God to give you the opportunity to share your faith today.

DEEP ROOTS

Blessed is the one whose delight is in the law of the L*ORD*, *and who meditates on his law day and night. That person is like a tree planted by streams of water, which yields its fruit in season and whose leaf does not wither—whatever they do prospers.* —Psalm 1:2–3 (NIV)

Last July, I was perusing a nursery for flowering trees to border my property when I found nine large pink crape myrtles for only $7 each. The catch was that it was the wrong time of year to plant trees. Not willing to pass up such a great deal, I loaded them up and brought them home.

After a few days of southern heat, I knew it would require determination to keep those trees alive until fall planting. I watered them three times daily and scrambled to upright the tall trees every time the wind blew. By the time the season changed, my trees were barely alive despite my hard work, and I was exhausted.

Once fall arrived, I was finally able to plant and water them one last time, knowing nature would take over. This spring, I saw that my endeavor had been successful. Each tree had grown taller and budded those stunning pink blooms.

Without God, I am like a large tree in a shallow pot that is thirsty, unstable, and susceptible to outside forces. When I delight in the Lord and meditate on His Word, I am immovable, with deep roots that are planted by streams of living water.

Lord, thank You for being my stability. You make whatever I do prosper. Amen.

—Jessi Creed

GROWING IN FAITH

Today find a large shady tree and think about its deep roots and that your delight in the Lord firmly plants your soul by His living water.

PLANTING SEEDS

But the seed in the good soil, these are the ones who have heard the word in an honest and good heart, and hold it fast, and bear fruit with perseverance. —Luke 8:15 (NASB1995)

One morning at our Bible study, we discussed how we sow seeds in the lives of our loved ones. For the members of our group, this meant spreading the good news of Jesus. One woman shared how she practices "withness" when she's in the presence of someone else. She immerses herself in that moment *with* that person. Another woman volunteers as a coach for a high school tennis team and opens her home for Bible study. Another shared that, just as seeds are small, she tries to be consistent with small acts of kindness with people she encounters every day.

All of these techniques for planting seeds reminded me of how similar gardening practices are to growing God's Kingdom. For my garden to flourish, I have to be present, knowing the condition of my plants. I also have to engage physically: I can't just talk about having a garden—I have to dig in. And I have to be consistent with small acts of tenderly nurturing my plants, such as trimming, fertilizing, and the never-ending weeding.

As we shared, I saw this group of women as Jesus's example of seeds that fell on good soil. They had each heard the word of Christ with honest and good hearts, held it fast, and persevered in planting seeds in the lives of others.

Lord, help me to be a faithful seed sower today, telling and showing others the love Jesus showed for me.
—Jeannie Blackmer

GROWING IN FAITH

What is one thing you can do today to plant a seed of love in someone else's life?

THE SMELL OF LILACS

I am come that they might have life, and that they might have it more abundantly. —John 10:10 (KJV)

As I pick up spent blossoms from a bouquet of lilacs, the small chore leaves a life lesson. At one time, my common knowledge was of two, maybe three, varieties of lilacs—white, light purple, and dark purple. Imagine then, how my heart soared when a friend invited me to a Lilac Extravaganza at an arboretum boasting more than 100 varieties of lilacs. The intoxicating fragrance of acre after acre of lilacs at their peak was only surpassed by the blossoms themselves. Pink, variegated, double ruffled, Japanese, French, rosy red, nearly black—so beautiful!

When my father died, my mother gifted me with a French lilac to plant on our property where I could see it every day. It grew slowly, but it's now full and filled with blossoms late in spring. Delicate, almost ethereal blossoms with that familiar, beautiful fragrance. They don't last as long as I'd like but they bring joy. And so did he.

Like so many things in life, what blooms beautifully doesn't necessarily last long. But rather than maintain a perpetual state of disappointment over that fact, it seems God may have wanted to remind me to enjoy what is short-lived fully. A stem of lilacs. Daffodils. Tulips. Grape hyacinths.

And those we have near us for fewer years than we hoped.

Lord, expand my horizons to wonders of Your creation around me… and both the beauty and people awaiting me in heaven. Amen.

—Cynthia Ruchti

GROWING IN FAITH

With tenderness, spend some time today thanking God for the lives of those you love who left a trail of fragrant spent blossoms.

OUTDOOR PRAYER ROOMS

Yet Jesus himself frequently withdrew to the wilderness and prayed.
—Luke 5:16 (NET)

When I was forty, I was diagnosed with a rare form of macular degeneration that is slowly making me lose my central vision. Bright light and high contrast are crucial to my ability to see well. That's one reason I spend lots of time outside in my garden.

This past year, my vision seems to have deteriorated rapidly. I can't help but feel fear as I worry about what the future holds for me. But in my garden, I find peace and joy despite my failing eyesight.

As much as I enjoy digging in the dirt, watching the butterflies flutter by, harvesting my fruits and vegetables, and seeing my colorful zinnias and other flowers, my real peace and joy comes from a deeper well and a more verdant garden.

In Matthew 6:6, Jesus told the people to enter their prayer rooms and close the door so they could pray to God alone, rather than putting on a show for others.

Jesus's prayer rooms were lonely and deserted places in the wilderness. Garden spaces are often my prayer rooms. Outdoors, I praise Him, lift up others' needs, express gratitude, listen for His voice, and confess my shortcomings. It's also where I turn my cares into prayers.

Sharing my fears and worries with the Lord focuses my attention where it needs to be—on Him.

Father, thank You for prayer gardens and for always being there.
With You I gain strength to meet life's challenges, and You turn
my worries into joy, contentment, and unsurpassable peace. Amen.
—Cathy Bryant

GROWING IN FAITH

Today, if the weather allows it, go outdoors to pray. If not, sit by a window and look outdoors before spending time with the Lord.

MAKING GOOD DIRT

Surely its life withers away, and from the soil other plants grow.
—Job 8:19 (NIV)

It has always seemed silly to me to throw stuff into the garbage that could better go elsewhere. Recyclables, for starters. Table scraps that pets can eat, for another. Where I live, there's no local landfill. Our county must pay by the pound for workers to haul our garbage away.

That's why I became a composter. In the backyard of the old farmhouse where I used to live was a feeding trough with a rusted-out bottom. I tossed kitchen scraps—minus meat, fat, and bones—into it. Occasionally, I added an armful of fallen leaves or grass clippings. When the spirit moved me, I stirred the contents of the trough with a pitchfork. God kept it watered. Thanks to the glorious soil this mess became, I grew some of the best vegetables and flowers imaginable.

When I moved to a different house, I couldn't take the trough. But the previous homeowner had left behind a metal wheelbarrow with several holes in it. That old wheelbarrow has become my new compost bin. Into it go banana peels, apple cores, eggshells, coffee grounds, and a whole lot of other organic matter that rots and becomes dirt. Just as I used to do with the feeding trough, I stir the contents of the wheelbarrow every now and then. God waters it. When planting time rolls around, I work this glorious compost into my flower beds and vegetable gardens.

And I rejoice when my healthy, happy plants reach toward the heavens.

Thank You, God, for the good dirt that makes life on earth possible.
—Jennie Ivey

GROWING IN FAITH

Search for ways to be a good steward of our planet and practice one today.

TO GROW . . . OR NOT

The righteous will flourish like a palm tree . . . They will still bear fruit in old age, they will stay fresh and green. —Psalm 92:12–14 (NIV)

The sun was warm on the front porch, and I settled into an Adirondack chair and placed my coffee mug on the nearby table next to the pot of impatiens. *Dead* impatiens. I plunked the mug down, splashing coffee.

I had noticed their lackluster appearance the day before, watered them, and hoped they'd perk up. But today they were worse. It was a partially shady spot, perfect for this flower. They had every opportunity, but they would not grow. The stems looked skeletal. Blooms curled oddly and had dropped withered petals.

This forlorn pot of dead flowers reminded me that growth is optional. Any of us can resist growth. As humans, we can get stuck for a long time. Some stay stuck for a lifetime. Strongholds can root deeply; generational patterns can train us to approach life and relationships—and God—in unhealthy ways.

But Jesus wants so much more than that for us.

Those impatiens did not make it, but they reminded me to pray for my heart and for others who need a transforming work from our Heavenly Father. His methods of healing never fail. He knows how to grow each of us in glorious ways.

If we aren't growing, we need to surrender to Him and learn to trust the unfailing hands of our Creator.

Father God, thank You for pursuing my growth.
Please help me surrender to Your care. Amen.
—Erin Keeley Marshall

GROWING IN FAITH

Today identify a part of your life that is wilted or seems to be dying. Ask God to bring it life.

FLOWER PAINTING

The heavens declare the glory of God; the skies proclaim the work of his hands. —Psalm 19:1 (NIV)

I've always considered myself an artist. I majored in art and spent a couple of decades traveling to art shows and dabbling in different mediums. When my life went in another direction and I stopping making art, I missed creating through color and expression.

On the flip side, I never considered myself a gardener. I've always joked about having a black thumb instead of a green one.

But then something clicked. I began to notice the variety of colors and the textures of the flowers and plants. I realized gardening is just as much of an art as painting with watercolors. Maybe more so because, unlike a still life, it's a living piece of art that changes from season to season.

Choosing which flowers to plant in a flower bed is similar to hovering a sable paintbrush over a palette, selecting the perfect color. Now when I see a flower, I no longer see a "red" flower; I see an alizarin crimson red, then picture how it would look with cadmium yellow or a touch of cerulean blue. I compare the silky texture of one type of petal to the complexity of another.

I found that just as art feeds my soul, gardening does too.

After all, God is the ultimate artist, and He provides the tools—seeds, flowers, sun, soil, and water—and then allows us to express ourselves on a small portion of His huge canvas, His vast masterpiece.

Thank You, Lord, that every day we see the glory of Your creation.

—Kristy Dewberry

GROWING IN FAITH

As you garden, picture your flower bed as God's canvas, a beautiful display of His love.

THE GIFT OF IRISES

Sweet friendships refresh the soul and awaken our hearts with joy.
—Proverbs 27:9 (TPT)

I pushed my spade into the ground and slowly lifted a clump of irises. I'd received these plants over the past two decades, but last spring only a handful of them bloomed. They'd become overcrowded. I needed to divide them again.

Irises are special to me because they've all found their way to my flower beds from friends and family. Double-blooming purple ones from Grandma Marge. Statuesque white beauties from Mariann, my mom's best friend. Bonnie, the mother of my ex-boss, gave me a petite lavender variety. Nana, my husband's grandmother, contributed bearded golden blossoms. And a coworker, Jennie, offered me some Superstition bearded iris—such a dark purple that they almost look black.

Each spring when they bloom, I remember with fondness the friends who shared their tubers with me. I marvel that these flowers have thrived in my flower beds as a living tribute to the women who gave them to me, even though all but one of these women have passed away. The simple gift of friendship in the form of flowers outlived their bodies—beautiful reminders of them and how each of us lives on through the legacy of our actions.

Recently, Jan, a friend from church, wanted some rhizomes. In the coming years, the gifts from my long-ago friends will bloom in the flower bed of a person they never met. A sweet reminder that friendship shared never dies.

Like these irises that were shared with me, Lord, let me pass on a heritage of generosity, kindness, and love to others. Amen.
—Stephanie Thompson

GROWING IN FAITH

As you thin out your flower bed or vegetable garden, gather a few rhizomes, seeds, or cuttings you've received from others to share with a friend.

It changes day by day and as each season unfolds, drifting gently or arriving urgently. Within a single day the garden can go through a hundred subtle nuances.

CAROL KLEIN, GARDENING EXPERT

ENSNARED BY BAD BEHAVIOR

"People are slaves to whatever has mastered them."
—2 Peter 2:19 (NIV)

After waiting in vain for some seeds to take root this year, I finally accepted the fact that I needed to supplement with annuals from the garden center. Getting them so late in the season meant the plants were root-bound when I removed them from the plastic trays. Although I'd been taught that you have to tear off the spiraling mass of roots at the bottom to stimulate the plant, it still felt a bit cruel to do so. Sure enough, though, it did the trick and the flowers took root and thrived.

I've had some seasons in my life when I've grown root-bound. I've gotten stuck in my ways with some patterns of bad behavior spiraling me in the wrong direction, over and over again, until life's sparkle and zeal got choked out in the process. Inevitably, something drastic would happen. What I knew and what seemed familiar would get torn away. I'd cry out to Jesus for help as I floundered about for where to put down new roots.

It feels cruel and painful at the time, but in retrospect, I can see how necessary this cutting away is and the good that comes from it. Moreover, Jesus is always with me through it all. No matter the discomfort, my Master Gardener knows when to remove what ensnares me, stimulating my growth so I can thrive.

Tender of Roots, when things are torn away, help me to develop new patterns that lead to new growth so I can thrive for You. Amen.
—Claire McGarry

GROWING IN FAITH

Identify one pattern you need to reverse.
Ask Jesus today to help you uproot it at the source.

FIXED ON GOD

But my eyes are fixed on you, Sovereign Lord; in you I take refuge.
—Psalm 141:8 (NIV)

Common folklore says that sunflowers always follow the sun, and scientists have proven that sunflowers *do*, all through their maturing season of growth. Overnight, the flowers turn their heads to the east so they will be facing that direction when the sun rises. Throughout the day, the head of the sunflower follows the trajectory of the sun through the sky to the west, overnight moving to face the east again.

I think sunflowers are a wonderful metaphor for our relationship with God. The Psalmist writes that his eyes are fixed on the Lord. So, too, the eye of the young sunflower is always fixed on the sun. In our youth, if we can keep our eyes on the Lord, then we will grow strong in our faith.

As the sunflower ages, it stops following the sun and simply faces east. This is because the flower now has shifted its focus from growth to pollination. Bees prefer warmer flowers, and the flower facing east gets the most daytime sun, grows the warmest, and attracts the most pollinators.

So, too, as we grow in faith, we become steadier. No longer do we need to cast about to the right and the left to find God. We are steady like the mature sunflower, facing one direction, standing tall and true.

The sunflowers in my garden are a wonderful reminder to keep my eyes fixed on the Lord.

Lord God, thank You for being a constant presence
in my life. My eyes are fixed on You.
—Heather Jepsen

GROWING IN FAITH

Throughout the day, keep aware of the position of the sun above you, thanking God for His light.

DIVINE MOMENTS

One generation commends your works to another;
they tell of your mighty acts. —Psalm 145:4 (NIV)

We bought our home from an elderly couple, Bob and Esther, who had to move into assisted living because Bob had been diagnosed with Alzheimer's. It was a tough decision for them to leave the house they had built fifty years before. Community-minded, Bob and Esther often had friends over for dinner and for ballroom dancing. They were also avid gardeners and had cultivated beautiful flower gardens around their home. We told them we intended to continue what they had started. We wanted to use this home as a place for community gatherings and would nurture the gardens they had established.

When the flowers started blooming the first year, I thought about Esther and how she must miss them. One that caught my eye was a peach rose whose color was astounding. I took a photo with my phone, said a silent prayer that this would bring her joy, and texted it to Esther. Immediately, she texted me back. "Thank you," she wrote. "This one is my favorite!"

I love when God aligns moments like this one. He knew Esther's favorite flower. I could have chosen to send her a picture of many others, but He directed me to the one that would most touch her heart. I also hoped this would assure her we were taking good care of the home they'd loved so much. Their labors were not forgotten but, rather, inspired us to follow in their footsteps.

Lord, thank You that Your works continue
from one generation to another. Amen.
—Jeannie Blackmer

GROWING IN FAITH

Take a photo of one of your favorite
plants or flowers and send it to a friend today.

EMBRACING PEACE

If it is possible, as far as it depends on you, live at peace with everyone.
—Romans 12:18 (NIV)

"Get out of here, you wascally wabbits!" I whisper-shouted in my best Elmer Fudd voice.

My pretend outrage at the bunnies lazily hopping around my backyard never fails to elicit laughter from my young neighbors. While it's funny to shake my fist in mock anger when young neighbors are watching, it was something else entirely to find a nest of newborn bunnies tucked into the middle of my fenced-in, supposedly rabbit-proof lettuce patch one morning.

You see, underlying my pretend anger lurks a very real annoyance with the damage rabbits inflict upon my garden, and it was at that moment of intense frustration that the Holy Spirit gently reminded me that rabbits aren't my enemy. Mama rabbit wasn't maliciously, repeatedly mowing down my tender pea shoots; she was just doing what bunnies do and, in the process, unintentionally causing me heartache.

Very few creatures are my actual enemies, including people. Most of the time, hurt is unintentionally inflicted through misunderstanding, carelessness, or inadvertence.

God loves the creatures I long to loathe. When I reframe my hurt feelings through that lens, I find compassion, grace, and forgiveness—for them *and* for me. That doesn't mean I don't reinforce my garden fence to keep bunnies out or have difficult conversations with those who have hurt me. But I do best when I remove the label "enemy" from others, replacing it with "child of God."

Heavenly Father, help me remember that those causing me hurt and frustration are Your beloved children.
—Julie Fisk

GROWING IN FAITH

Identify any unforgiveness in your life. Bring it to God in prayer, asking for help as you release it.

IN NEED OF DEADHEADING

"Forget the former things; do not dwell on the past. See, I am doing a new thing! Now it springs up; do you not perceive it?"
—Isaiah 43:18–19 (NIV)

My sister is obsessed with deadheading flowers, and not just the flowers at her house. No, she's been known to jump out of the car in the drive-through line and deadhead a pot of begonias in front of a fast-food restaurant. I think it's because she is a designer by trade, so her eyes are trained to notice every detail. She simply can't rest until all of the ugly, dry, dead parts of a plant are removed, making room for beautiful new blossoms. I always appreciate it when she deadheads the flowers at my house.

Let's face it: we all need a little deadheading once in a while. And I'm not talking about flowers. Spiritually speaking, we need God to remove the old, ugly mindsets that keep us from moving forward into the beautiful plans He has for us. I mean those old recordings that tell us, "You're not good enough. Nobody likes you. God doesn't care about you. He could never use you."

Next time those old recordings begin playing, follow my sister's example and start deadheading.

Better yet, ask God—the Master Gardener—to help you remove the old and make room for the new.

Your beautiful new life awaits.

Heavenly Father, please remove those old, ugly mindsets and make way for the new things You want to do in me and through me. I love You. Amen.
—Michelle Medlock Adams

GROWING IN FAITH

It's impossible to fight a thought with a thought. So when that old recording of lies begins playing in your mind, say what the Word of God says about you.

LAVENDER MEMORIES

Then Samuel took a stone and set it up between Mizpah and Shen. He named it Ebenezer, saying, "Thus far the LORD has helped us."
—1 Samuel 7:12 (NIV)

Silvery-green leaves pushed up through the dirt. Over the next weeks, tall shoots sprouted and then fragrant pale purple blossoms appeared, swaying in the wind. I'd planted this lavender plant the previous year because it reminded me of France—and now it was back and blooming again!

I plucked a frond and inhaled, and my shoulders instantly relaxed. Images of the French countryside, cobblestone streets, and tiny cafes filled my mind. One whiff of this plant transported me to my favorite place on earth and reminded me of the ways God had blessed me there. Each time I pass my lavender plant, I smile, recalling God's goodness.

God gives us so many ways to remember what He's done for us, where He's taken us, and the people He's brought into our lives, but do we take time to remember? When God helped the Israelites win a battle they shouldn't have won, the prophet Samuel set up a stone and named it Ebenezer, "the stone of help," so all could recall what God had done.

God takes care of us and answers our prayers, and we're grateful, but sometimes just for a moment. We then go about living our lives again, forgetting His kindness. Creating our own Ebenezers can help us recall God's goodness and faithfulness, renewing our trust and hope for the future.

Dear God, please help me to pause and remember all the times You've been there for me. Amen.
—Laura L. Smith

GROWING IN FAITH

Is there a plant that helps you remember a blessing? Its scent, flavor, or bloom? Plant it today as your own Ebenezer of God's faithfulness.

CLEANING OUT FOR THE GOOD

Turn from evil and do good; seek peace and pursue it.
—Psalm 34:14 (NIV)

I was a sucker for volunteers. I also hated thinning out seedlings, so when volunteers sprouted all over my garden, I didn't yank up a single one. Veggies from last year mixed with several plants I didn't recognize, with lacy foliage and tiny purple flowers.

As the season progressed, my garden became a jumbled jungle. Then, a green-thumbed neighbor took a look. He gently pointed out that if I wanted a harvest, I'd need to make room for the plants I actually wanted.

"And these," he said, pointing to the lacy plants, "are nightshade relatives."

He uprooted one and held it under my nose.

What a stench! I hadn't wanted to eliminate volunteers. Now they strangled everything. And what I'd thought was a pretty plant was a noxious weed. The neighbor helped me clean up my little plot and thinned the crowded carrots. I took his advice, thankful for his wisdom.

Later, as I tended neat rows of lettuce, spinach, and kale, I thought about the many ways I sometimes allow life to be overrun by trivial details and distracted by alluring, but stinking, thinking.

This year, I'll thin my seedlings and kick out shady upstarts.

And when I'm tempted to let any old volunteer blossom in me, I'll remember that God is like my gentle neighbor, patiently showing me how growing good and nourishing faith often means the unhelpful stuff has to go.

Father, help me grow in goodness and teach me to uproot any evil that begins to grow in me.

—Linda S. Clare

GROWING IN FAITH

Thinning seedlings requires a gentle hand. Today, when you become aware of a mistake you've made, accept God's mercy and be gentle with yourself.

ROOTED

"For I am the LORD your God who takes hold of your right hand and says to you, Do not fear; I will help you." —Isaiah 41:13 (NIV)

My son Samuel found me in the garden.

"Let me help," he said. He knelt beside me as we pulled weeds.

"Have you thought about it?" he asked. "May I go?"

Sam was eighteen and college-bound in the fall. That afternoon, he wanted to go to the lake with friends. But the lake is a flooded forest, and swimming could be dangerous. Years before, another adventurous young son had been trapped in a cave for twenty-one hours. The memory haunted me.

I pulled a weed but didn't answer Samuel's question.

"The basil looks great," he said. "It's grown a lot."

It had.

We'd started the herbs from seeds in little brown planting cups. When they were strong enough to be planted outdoors, I'd peeled the cup away to place the plant in the earth. The roots were tiny and tangled but strong. Strong enough to anchor the herbs.

Just like the Lord anchored me.

His Word provided me with a root system strong enough to hold in times of worry. But I had to choose that anchoring, to remember the roots, and to believe that the Lord would do what He said He'd do.

And He said that He'd help me.

Sam stopped weeding and looked at me with wide green eyes.

"I know that you worry, Mom," he said. "But I'm careful."

Fear cannot uproot a soul tethered to truth.

My garden helper left that day to swim, but my holy Helper stayed.

Lord, help me when fear comes close. Amen.

—Shawnelle Eliasen

GROWING IN FAITH

Today replace one worry with anchoring words of truth.

DIFFERENT KIND OF DIFFERENT

But let each one examine his own work, and then he will have rejoicing in himself alone, and not in another. —Galatians 6:4 (NKJV)

My sister-in-law's garden is different from mine. Her yard and flower beds are lush with palms and tropical plants and something is always blooming. On a recent visit, I marveled that the holly I pay dearly for at Christmas in the Northwoods grows hedge-high in her front yard. Plants I've never seen before—like her French mulberry—show their prolific beauty as if unaware how stunning they are. A banana tree, complete with baby bananas, grows outside her kitchen window.

This is not the kind of foliage found in my neck of the literal woods. Gardeners like me study seed catalogs looking for short spans of time between planting and harvest, discarding the idea of any vegetables or other plants that can't fully mature between mid-May and late August. In our area, July is the only month that through history has escaped having at least one snowfall. We've even run the furnace in August.

How foolish it would be if I were to measure the worth of my garden against my sister-in-law's. They're two different things. We're in two different growing zones and experience differing temperatures, humidity levels, and soil types. What works for my sister-in-law won't work for me and vice versa.

Thank you, garden.

And thank You, God, for yet another lesson from Creation.

Father, keep me attuned to the beauty in differences and variety, rather than stuck in the futility and fruitlessness of comparison. Amen.

—Cynthia Ruchti

GROWING IN FAITH

Do you compare yourself or your life to others? Today spend time in prayer, asking God to lift that burden from you so you can better appreciate what He has given you.

A SMALL, SACRED LIFE

Then the L*ORD* *God took the man and put him in the garden of Eden to tend and keep it.* —Genesis 2:15 (NKJV)

It's break time. I water the herbs, refresh my teacup, and pet the cat. When I return to my tiny home office, a job posting has slithered into my email. The glamorous-sounding opportunity is something for which I qualify, the same sort of work I now do remotely. But in that position, I'd be seen and appreciated. Maybe even admired.

For the millionth time, I question, "Is my life enough? Does my work matter less because it's unseen? Did it matter back when I nursed babies, read to toddlers, helped with homework? Does it matter now when I vacuum?"

If my life were a garden, it would be a *garth*. Garth happens to be my husband's name, and it's an ancient term meaning a small enclosed yard or garden. Simple. Modest.

I contrast this with the elaborate grounds of a seventeenth-century Italian villa I once toured. With its acres of well-manicured azaleas and rhododendrons, citrus tunnels, and elegant fountains, this garden was fit for a princess. In fact, in 1850 the villa was presented as a wedding gift to Princess Carlotta of Prussia. Countless hands fuss over Villa Carlotta's upkeep. Myriad visitors admire it.

And yet I know that this small and sacred life God assigned to me matters too. Because it matters to Him.

I delete the "opportunity" email. If God admires my humble garth, that's good enough for me.

Lord, I sense Your pleasure when I faithfully tend and keep my life's garden. Help me remain satisfied. Amen.

—Kit Tosello

GROWING IN FAITH

From your to-do list, select a tedious chore. Perform it today with joyfulness and reverence as an act of worship.

GIVING GOD THE CREDIT

So neither the one who plants nor the one who waters is anything, but only God, who makes things grow. The one who plants and the one who waters have one purpose, and they will each be rewarded according to their own labor. For we are co-workers in God's service; you are God's field, God's building. —1 Corinthians 3:7–9 (NIV)

"Grandpa, Grandpa!" my neighbor's grandson, Max, called. "Audrey says the cherry tomatoes are hers because she waters them every time she comes to visit. Tell her that they are mine because I helped you plant the seeds last winter!"

Max's small voice carried from my neighbor's yard to where I bent tending my own garden, harvesting my own first ripe tomatoes.

Smiling, I listened as my neighbor, Jerry, navigated the conflict between his young grandchildren with gentle explanation and redirection, explaining that while they each helped with a part of the process, neither gets to claim all the credit *or* all the harvest.

My thoughts turned to my own periodically misplaced feelings of accomplishment. Just as Audrey and Max wanted to claim credit because of the small roles they played in the tomatoes' growth, I sometimes try to claim credit for my small role in God's plans—whether in the lives of people I love, in the acts of service I perform as the hands and feet of Christ, or even in my own garden as I proudly harvest what God has grown.

Heavenly Father, show me where I try to claim glory when all of the glory is Yours. Forgive me for my arrogance and sin.

—Julie Fisk

GROWING IN FAITH

Where might you be inadvertently taking the credit for God's handiwork when you are merely His coworker? Seek forgiveness and a new, clearer perspective.

GARDEN REVERIE

You make known to me the path of life; you will fill me with joy in your presence, with eternal pleasures at your right hand. —Psalm 16:11 (NIV)

Oh, how lovely are the melodies of my garden reverie! Come along with me. Experience God's splendorous blessings on this day—my daydreaming, my musings, my spiritual connections and conversations with the earth. I am not a poet, nor do I dress like one in blouses of puffy poet sleeves. But this space feels nonetheless overwhelmingly poetic and spiritual, a glimpse of heaven here on earth.

A winding brick path passes a row of burning bushes dressed in their flickering emerald summer leaves. The nannyberry attracts birds to its creamy white flowers. Arching over the garden gate entrance is a show-stopper clematis, a symphony of stunning velvety purple.

A sight to behold, countless perennials are crowded shoulder to shoulder, supporting each other's stems, living together in peace and harmony, as God wishes for us.

The only annual is the centerpiece, a red Dragon Wing begonia, a non-stop bloomer. A banquet of flowering colors and foliage in every shade of green. Around it, daisies, lilies of the valley, irises, daffodils, peonies, pansies, and much more—all symbols of beauty and grace, glorious reminders of the miracles of His creation. Species of every size and color under heaven.

Peace radiates as hummingbirds, bees, and butterflies busy themselves, dancing and singing the praises of this garden feast. Surely the presence of the Lord is in this place.

Heavenly Father, thank You for Your goodness and
our gardens to remind us of Your love.
—Cookie Cranston

GROWING IN FAITH

Today look with wonder on some part of God's creation,
whether a tree, a cloud, or stars in the night sky.
Thank God for His presence.

A garden is a grand teacher. It teaches patience and careful watchfulness; it teaches industry and thrift; above all it teaches entire trust.

GERTRUDE JEKYLL, BRITISH GARDEN DESIGNER AND HORTICULTURIST

IN THE HARD SOIL

"At least there is hope for a tree: If it is cut down, it will sprout again, and its new shoots will not fail."
—Job 14:7 (NIV)

After an arduous wait for spring's thaw, on a May morning warmed by an eager sun, my four kids and I get our hands dirty. Thirty starter plants from our "Colorado Oasis" native plant garden kit wait for a new home in our garden plot. It is no small task dredging up the rock-hard—and rock-filled—soil of the Colorado prairie. I have my doubts that anything can grow in these unfavorable conditions. Shouldn't a garden be full of rich, dark, wet-smelling soil, the kind that feels cool to the touch and soft on the fingertips? Instead, we engage all our muscles to flip up chunks of dry, hot, caked-together earth. We press root clumps into imperfect, jagged-edged holes in hopes that our efforts will be worthwhile.

Spring planting is always therapeutic, yet this act of hand-tilling hard soil feels even more significant after a difficult season. Like the harsh conditions of winter on this stubborn soil, recent circumstances have left my heart feeling resistant to growth.

But God is working here, right beside me in the garden, never giving up on my obstinate heart and assuring me that right in the hard soil is where He brings forth abiding growth and beauty.

Lord, what I see as a lost cause, You see as opportunity. You are actively tilling the resistant soil of my spirit. Grow me here in the hard soil.
—Eryn Lynum

GROWING IN FAITH

Is there a situation you've hesitated to trust God with? Bring it to Him in an honest prayer and ask Him to grow you in that hard place.

TRAINING VINES

All Scripture is God-breathed and is useful for teaching, rebuking, correcting and training in righteousness. —2 Timothy 3:16 (NIV)

Although I've planted cucumbers many times, this year was my first time growing them on a fence. What a positive difference it made, especially in the amount of produce. As with all my vegetables that grow on vines—beans, grapes, tomatoes, and squash—I had to take the time to train the cucumbers. I wove part of the plant around the fence, training it to climb and grow there. No matter how often and patiently I repeated this process, there were always some vines that refused to stay put, snaking along the ground instead, where they were easily stepped on and broken, their fruit easy for garden pests to damage.

In the Old Testament, many references are made to God's people being like wayward vines.

And I can be that way too. Like the vines in my garden, I'm sometimes unruly and wayward, refusing to be trained. This happens most often when I get so busy that I'm not spending time reading the Bible. Without the training His Word provides, I put myself in spiritual danger and my productivity for His Kingdom dwindles.

Thankfully, the Lord is quick to woo me back into His Word, gently drawing me closer to Him so that I can grow strong and bear good fruit.

Father, forgive my tendency to sometimes wander away from You and Your training. Help me to spend time daily in Scripture and apply it to my life. Amen.

—Cathy Bryant

GROWING IN FAITH

Spend time today reading a favorite psalm or other passage in the Bible. Consider choosing a time every day for reading God's Word.

KNEE-HIGH BY THE FOURTH OF JULY

Rejoice always, pray continually, give thanks in all circumstances; for this is God's will for you in Christ Jesus. —1 Thessalonians 5:16–18 (NIV)

Knee-high by the Fourth of July: That's what I'd always heard about a good corn crop. So imagine my surprise when my husband, Bill, and I planted sweet corn for the first time in our Kentucky backyard, and it shot up over our heads and shoulders by Independence Day.

Giddy with glee, we decided to host a "corn boil" party later that summer when our crop was ready to harvest. We planned to invite all our friends and neighbors. Then came the unexpected summer storm that flattened the towering cornstalks. Our hearts sank, and I cried.

In the first letter to the Thessalonians, Paul admonishes believers to give thanks to God in *all* circumstances. We did, despite our disappointment, recognizing that His grace is sufficient for us.

A few days later, there was another storm—mostly wind that rattled the windows during the night. Imagine our surprise the next morning when we discovered our corn standing straight and tall once again! Our neighbor declared she'd never seen anything like it. Neither had we.

Several weeks later, our backyard was filled with guests drinking sweet tea and eating buttery corn on the cob. They, too, were amazed when we walked them into the field to point out the odd kink near the bottom of each stalk—evidence that the corn had been flattened, then straightened—evidence that our God can do anything!

Heavenly Father, we praise You for Your loving-kindness, recognizing You as our creator and sustainer. Amen.

—Shirley Raye Redmond

GROWING IN FAITH

Make a list today of times when God has granted your heart's desire. Thank Him.

JUST DO IT

No discipline seems pleasant at the time, but painful. Later on, however, it produces a harvest of righteousness and peace for those who have been trained by it. —Hebrews 12:11 (NIV)

I neglected my flower beds, and now I regretted it. If I'd started pulling those little green sprouts when they broke through the soil last month, it wouldn't be so overwhelming. For at least six weeks, I'd been watching the weeds grow like, well, weeds. I berated myself for having put it off. I made excuses for myself. I'd been too busy. I was too tired. It was too cold.

But was I really just lazy?

I haven't always been a procrastinator. Through the years, I've found clarity or heard from God when my fingers were in the dirt. So why did I *put off until tomorrow what I could do today* when it came to pulling weeds? I resolved to turn my *maybe later* slogan into *just do it*. I made a date with my spade for the weekend.

Saturday at 8 a.m., I pulled on my gardening gloves and carried my caddy to the far end of the flower bed. Praise music played over the outdoor speakers. Breathing in the fresh summer air renewed my mind and encouraged my soul. I actually felt *happy* doing the job I'd avoided and even dreaded for more than a month.

After a few hours, I marveled at the progress I'd made.

I realized that I'd spent much more time procrastinating over what I knew I should do than it actually took to accomplish it.

Lord, please give me discipline that overcomes procrastination in all areas of my life. Amen.
—Stephanie Thompson

GROWING IN FAITH

Today identify one task you've been avoiding and take one small step toward accomplishing it.

DAILY MERCY

The Lord's lovingkindnesses indeed never cease... They are new every morning. —Lamentations 3:22–23 (NASB1995)

My northern grandmother's neighborhood in Rhode Island smelled of salt spray, roses, and, if the wind blew right, fresh-baked Italian bread. My southern grandmother's neighborhood swirled with scents of warm pine, honeysuckle, and fried chicken.

On vacation, I stretched out on my southern Granny's guest bed to read an ancient copy of *Reader's Digest.* A slight breeze rustled the curtains, bringing with it a scent I didn't recognize. I peered out the window and saw a patch of hot pink flowers blooming in the shade of the house.

"Four-o'clocks," Granny said when I asked.

I buried my face in the fragrant blossoms, then picked a handful. Placing them in a mason jar on my dresser, I anticipated enjoying them all week. Sadly, when I checked them the next morning, the flowers had shriveled up. I tossed them in the trash and picked a new bunch later that afternoon when the scent again wafted through the window. The next day, they were dead.

"What's with these flowers?" I asked Granny.

She laughed. "They're like daylilies," she said. "The blossoms only last one day. But don't worry, new flowers will appear again tomorrow."

Four-o'clocks are a lot like God's mercy. The flowers remind me that regardless of what I face each day, God promises to supply a fresh measure of mercy, grace, and love to help me through it. And He'll be there for me again tomorrow.

Thank You, Father, for providing exactly what I need every day. Amen.
—Lori Hatcher

GROWING IN FAITH

Today, when you begin to worry about the future, stop yourself and instead look around, right where you are. What do you *see, smell, taste* of God's love?

FILLING THE GAPS

My help comes from the LORD, the Maker of heaven and earth.
—Psalm 121:2 (NIV)

I built a raised flower bed this spring that runs along the curve of my driveway. Some of the pavers I used needed to be cut to accommodate the turn. I'm no stone mason, and I don't own a rock-cutting saw. Too impatient to stop and seek the help of a professional, I left gaps in the wall and covered them from the inside with cardboard. It was good enough to hold the soil in place so I could plant. Do you know it's more than four months later and I still haven't had those pavers cut? The cardboard is starting to rot, allowing soil to spill out onto my driveway.

How often do I approach life like this? How often do I feel completely capable of taking on a new challenge and attempt to keep all the control myself? Even when I recognize my need for help, I find work-arounds to forge ahead.

God made me incomplete so I'd turn to Him, and to others, for help. I'm not meant to do life alone, fudging my way through things that aren't in my wheelhouse. I have a Savior waiting to partner with me. He's always offering a lasting solution, not one that just holds things at bay for a while before breaking down, letting my shortcomings spill out.

Jesus is a jack-of-all-trades and a master of everything. I need to bring Him my stones to cut and my gaps to fill. When I do, I'll reap the reward of finally being complete.

Wonderful Counselor, inspire me to turn to
You for help with all that I need. Amen.
—Claire McGarry

GROWING IN FAITH
Ask someone for help today,
and lean into Jesus to fill your gaps.

GROWING ROOTS

Happy are those who reject the advice of evil people, who do not follow the example of sinners or join those who have no use for God. Instead, they find joy in obeying the Law of the LORD, and they study it day and night. They are like trees that grow beside a stream, that bear fruit at the right time, and whose leaves do not dry up. They succeed in everything they do.

—Psalm 1:1–3 (GNT)

My green-thumbed mom taught me that placing flowerpots by the front door gives a house a "wow" factor. This year, I planted bright red geraniums paired with coleus in my pots. The coleus took off, over-crowding my geraniums with their thick green and purple leaves.

My mom suggested trimming back the coleus, putting the cuttings in water until they grew roots, then replanting them. I snipped off large stems of coleus and placed them in water. My geraniums were visible again, and two weeks later the coleus clippings had stringy roots. I replanted the stems, unsure of how they'd do, but they thrived! I don't get any credit. Coleus grows roots when it's put in water; it's just what it does.

Psalm 1 tells us those who delight in the Scriptures are like trees planted by water. When we sink our broken selves into the Bible and plant ourselves in His Word, we grow roots. We gain strength. Instead of shriveling, we thrive.

Jesus, thank You for the Bible to help us grow roots,
strengthen our souls, and thrive. Amen.

—Laura L. Smith

GROWING IN FAITH

Set aside a consistent time to read your Bible every day this week. Not sure where to start? How about the Psalms?

POWER OF WORDS

The tongue has the power of life and death, and those who love it will eat its fruit. —Proverbs 18:21 (NIV)

Recently, my husband came home from helping a friend in the landscaping business with a truckload of unwanted, withered plants he "saved." Excited by the prospect of enhancing my landscaping for free, I accepted the challenge of rehabilitating the Kong coleus, petunias, and Silver Falls dichondra plants.

Although I was new to gardening, I knew they needed water and proper sunlight. As I arranged them in the dirt around my house, God reminded me of the power of my words. As I watered each pitiful plant, I would speak of its beauty and how glorious it would grow to be.

At first, it felt unnatural to look through eyes of faith and speak the opposite of what I was seeing. As time progressed, though, I was pleased to watch my plants grow until they had abundant, beautiful blooms and foliage.

I could have told my husband that I didn't want those sickly plants. But I made the choice to nourish them instead, and through God's demonstration, I discovered the power of words in creating life or death. It got me thinking about how many times my words have held anger, frustration, disappointment, and judgment rather than love and acceptance.

I learned a valuable life lesson in tending those plants—positivity causes us to flourish, whereas negativity makes us wither. Rather than being critical of myself and others, I now intentionally think and speak words of life, just as God's Word of life intends.

God, please renew my mind to see through faith-filled eyes. Amen.

—Jessi Creed

GROWING IN FAITH

Today be a light by using your thoughts and words to cultivate life in every circumstance.

FLOURISHING WHERE I'M PLANTED

The righteous will thrive like a green leaf. —Proverbs 11:28 (NIV)

I knew this was a long-game approach. Two months ago, sowing scraggly, not-much-to-look-at root balls into our garden, I didn't hold out much hope for blooms this season.

"Year one, they sleep," our printed garden guide told us. "Year two, they creep; year three, they leap!" Perhaps in three years, spring would greet us with a thriving pollinator garden. Then, maybe, butterflies, bees, and birds would mark our backyard as an important stopover on their journeys.

However, in the weeks following our planting, we witnessed what felt like a miracle. These native plants, meant to thrive in the dry, arid conditions of the desert, took root and quickly began filling in the gaps between one another. Red prairie coneflowers were the most eager of them all, enthusiastically shooting stems toward the sky and unfurling into crimson red petals. Blue harebell followed, gracing the garden with soft purple bells drooping from lanky stems. Firecracker penstemon lit up the garden with tall stalks boasting fluorescent red blossoms. Curious bees began to visit, along with flies and moths.

What I saw as harsh conditions were exactly what these plants needed to thrive. Similarly, God wants to grow me right where I'm planted. He meets my every need, and no matter the circumstances, enables me to thrive and flourish by His grace and in His provisions.

Lord, You are well aware of my circumstances. You have created me to thrive where I'm planted. Help me to trust You for everything I need.

—Eryn Lynum

GROWING IN FAITH

What difficult circumstance is sapping your joy or leaving your faith parched? Bring this situation to God today and ask Him to help you thrive right where you are.

REJOICE IN THE DAY

This is the day that the LORD has made; let us rejoice and be glad in it.
—Psalm 118:24 (ESV)

We have a flower patch just off the patio of the west side of our home. I kept the roses and other plants the couple who lived here before us had grown and added a few perennials. During our first spring, each flower that bloomed was a delightful surprise. In one corner stood a thick, stalky plant. I didn't know what it was. No one I asked knew what it was either. Because it looked ugly, I kept cutting the stalks down, but the plant kept growing back. Finally, I gave up and let it grow. In July, beautiful pink tropical flowers the size of small dinner plates bloomed. It turned out to be a hibiscus plant.

I never imagined hibiscus could thrive in Colorado. As I delved deeper into this exotic flower with showy foliage, I discovered there are two types of hibiscus: a tropical variety and a hardy variety. The hardy hibiscus tolerates harsh, cold winters, and I felt I'd won the lottery with this lovely flower blooming in my garden.

Each hibiscus flower only blooms for one day. Every morning, I look at the pink flowers and feel glad for the beauty they bring to my life that day. I think this is how God wants us to live too: day by day, rejoicing in the gift of a new day, and spreading gladness to those we encounter.

Lord, thank You for today. Help me to rejoice
and be glad in each and every day.
—Jeannie Blackmer

GROWING IN FAITH

Read Ephesians 5:15–16, which advises us to make good use of the time we have. Journal about how you can do this.

Through gardening, we feel whole as we make our personal work of art upon our land.

JULIE MOIR MESSERVY,
LANDSCAPE DESIGNER

MAKING LASAGNA

Therefore we do not lose heart. Though outwardly we are wasting away, yet inwardly we are being renewed day by day. —2 Corinthians 4:16 (NIV)

With our clay soil, I worried that growing a vegetable garden might not be possible. Besides, I'd grown up in the Arizona desert and was a novice gardener. I'd just about given up hope for a garden of my own when my neighbor introduced a novel way for me to get started, despite such sticky clay soil.

He called it "lasagna gardening." Instead of digging, I'd *build* a garden by piling soil, compost, and mulch on top of a base of newspapers or cardboard. No matter how hard and compact the earth underneath, these layers would become a rich, loose soil.

I followed his instructions and then, prayerfully, tucked in my seedlings and seeds. I watered and tended the plants, marveling at how few weeds sprang up through the mulch. I chopped up leaves and spread old coffee grounds on my garden, along with sawdust and wood ashes.

Over the course of the summer, I grew a bumper crop of beans, potatoes, lettuces, carrots, and beets. Yes, it was hard work. But every single day, I got to hang out with God, praying and singing as I got my hands dirty. I praised God for new life and the good things He brings.

Layer by layer, as I "lasagna garden," my faith and love of God are also bursting to life.

Lord, thank You for making new ways for us to thrive.
—Linda S. Clare

GROWING IN FAITH

What problem in your life (or your garden) seems impossible? Today brainstorm new ways to solve it. Let God expand your horizons as you step out in faith.

ODE TO A DAISY

The LORD is my strength and my defense; he has become my salvation.
—Exodus 15:2 (NIV)

Oh, the splendor of those flashy, floating white petals, placed around the bright yellow center disk of florets. Spiking from slender, glossy green foliage, the beautiful daisy! Prolific and growing without effort wherever her seeds land—gardens, fields, even cracks in concrete.

My small garden is an orchard of flower stems and petals. But how lovely is a garden that shows off a sea of white daisies, floating in waves and sailing on ripples in the breeze.

Daisies, their name derived from "day's eye," open every morning and close each night. Their opening and closing reminds me of the beauty of God's creation and of His redemption for us. Each day we start anew, just like a daisy's florets. They are thought to symbolize purity and new beginnings, and bees love to pollinate them.

Like us, daisies need nutrients to survive. Their adaptive nature allows them to cheerfully thrive in drought or wet conditions, in small clumps in gardens or in single stems in high meadows, just as God watches over our environment and cares for us.

I am not a poet, but if I watch and listen carefully, whether in the garden or in a mountain meadow, daisies' presence feels like poetry. Faith and peace resonate from the flutter of their tiny white petals and from the wings of the tiny white butterflies that visit them.

I am grateful to God for placing us in safe environments in which to grow and bloom too.

Father, thank You for the miracles that beautify our gardens!
—Cookie Cranston

GROWING IN FAITH

Look at a daisy today, whether in your garden or in a picture. Reflect on its simple beauty. Know that God views you, too, with wonder and love.

BROKEN BRANCHES

He heals the brokenhearted and binds up their wounds.
—Psalm 147:3 (NIV)

"Hi, Darlin'. How are you?" my dad asked. He stood up to hug me.

"I'm okay, Dad," I said. Chair legs scraped floorboards, and we sat down on his back porch. I was worried that day about my young adult son; a hurt he'd experienced ached in my own chest.

The yard of my childhood home was a comfort to me. The towering pine was once a sapling in a coffee can that I'd brought home from grade school. The vegetable garden sprawled over the back corner.

"The porch plants are doing pretty well," Dad said. "But this little guy was damaged by the wind."

Recently, Mom and Dad kept a few plants close to the house, closer than those in the big garden. Now he reached for the young cherry tomato plant near his chair. A branch dangled, limp and broken.

I noticed electrical tape and scissors on the table.

"I believe I can mend it," he said.

I'd watched Dad fix things all my life. Cars. Clocks. Appliances. And the tender way he handled the branch that day touched my soul. Dad cut a thin strip of tape and wound it around, lifting and securing the branch to the stem. My spirit lifted, too, as understanding settled in my soul.

The Lord is binder of the broken.

My son was in His care.

"There we go," my dad said. His hands folded in his lap as he admired his work. "This one's going to be okay."

And I knew he was right.

Father, I praise You because You see our hurts and offer help in healing. Amen.
—Shawnelle Eliasen

GROWING IN FAITH

If there's a broken branch in your life today, lift it to the Lord, knowing He can mend it.

LITTLE SUCKERS EVERYWHERE

Therefore, since we are surrounded by such a great cloud of witnesses, let us throw off everything that hinders and the sin that so easily entangles.
—Hebrews 12:1 (NIV)

As a novice gardener, I'd managed to plant about a thousand square feet, a more than an adequate patch for my young family. To my delight, everything sprouted and thrived.

The tomatoes, especially, were my pride and joy. Thanks to a secret weapon—well-aged manure acquired from a nearby farm—the vines had become exceptionally lush. Within a short time, they'd covered the trellises I'd built. Blossoms abounded!

"What do you think of these?" I asked my gardening mentor, a retired farmer.

"Not bad," he said, his tone less enthusiastic than I'd hoped. "But you need to get rid of them suckers."

Sucker vines, I learned, were nonfruit-bearing shoots from the main vine. Once I noticed them, they seemed to be *everywhere*. Darker green than the rest, with larger leaves, they were healthy. And useless. I lopped them off as quickly as I could.

Now that I know what to look for, I see these suckers elsewhere in life: impressive wastes of time and energy. They feel good and often feed my ego. But they do nothing to advance my intimacy with Christ. In fact, they detract from it.

Without the sucker vines, my tomato plants looked a bit scraggly, almost sickly. Yet they produced bushels of ripe red tomatoes.

My life seems smaller without *spiritual* suckers too. And it bears more fruit.

Lord Jesus, help me to value the things that truly matter and take my praise only from You.
—Lawrence W. Wilson

GROWING IN FAITH

Identify one thing that draws your attention away from Jesus and toward yourself. Then press "delete."

A WIND-TOSSED SEED

And if God cares so wonderfully for wildflowers . . . he will certainly care for you. —Matthew 6:30 (NLT)

My daughter seemed determined to wander a destructive path. Worries for her safety weighed heavily on me. Perhaps a long walk would ease my nerves and shake loose the right words to pray.

I rounded a corner, following the sidewalk along a tidy red fence. My path converged with a giant sunflower. I craned my neck to admire its bright, golden face, tilted toward the sun. But what was it doing here, on the wrong side of someone's fence?

Just as I lifted my camera to snap a photo, a white-haired man emerged from behind the fence. He beamed with pride, eager to share the story. His prize—and surprise—sunflower had gotten its start from a seed that drifted into a tiny mound of manure just outside his fence. "Imagine my delight!" he said. "So I ran a drip line from my garden."

A peek into his yard revealed rows of flourishing flowers and vegetables. Clearly, the gentleman was a master gardener. Yet this single flower, this golden surprise, was all he wanted to talk about.

Peace descended from seeing the tender care this man showed for a wayward seed and reminding me that my Master Gardener cares for me. And my daughter. No matter where she might wander, God loves and delights in her!

Thank You, God, that prayer doesn't always require words. Amen.

—Kit Tosello

GROWING IN FAITH

Close your eyes and imagine you're carrying a heavy basket overflowing with today's worries. You come upon a garden gate. Now open it and enter. Hand your burden to the Master Gardener—the one with kind eyes, outstretched arms, and nail-scarred hands.

TENDERIZING THE HEART

"A good man out of the good treasure of his heart brings forth good; and an evil man out of the evil treasure of his heart brings forth evil. For out of the abundance of the heart his mouth speaks." —Luke 6:45 (NKJV)

I try to remove a few weeds from my rose garden every morning. Otherwise, the weeds accumulate and an hour of pulling won't even make a dent.

My plan works great if we get regular rain showers, but after a few days of dry weather the sun hardens the ground. Then my attempts at unearthing the weeds fail. They break off from the top, and I can't get to the roots.

The same is true for my heart. I become desensitized to sin when I'm not bathed in God's Word. I get dried out, and I hear myself speak with a sharpness that startles my senses. Even when I keep angry or negative words and thoughts to myself, I feel a heaviness in my heart. An absence of peace.

Like pouring rain softens the ground, God softens my heart. As I read Scripture, pray, and worship, I can sense His presence, conviction, and love. My tender heart heeds His warnings. My tongue replies to others with kindness, and my heart is filled with the peace of His presence.

Father, thank You for tenderizing my heart to Your voice. Help me to not neglect my time with You. Fill my heart to overflowing that all I do may honor You. Amen.

—Crystal Storms

GROWING IN FAITH

What things of God soften your heart?
Today engage with at least one of them.

EMBRACE WHO YOU ARE

We have different gifts, according to the grace given to each of us.
—Romans 12:6 (NIV)

In my early years of homeownership, I planted my favorite annuals in my yard. Hot pink impatiens in my sunny front beds. Lily of the valley in my east-facing window boxes. Variegated hostas around the west-facing mailbox.

Some plants died a swift and dramatic death, turning yellow, then brown, then crispy. Others languished for a while, panting in the hot South Carolina sun before they expired.

"Maybe the soil is bad," I commented to my florist mother-in-law.

She shook her head and smiled.

"You can't plant shade-loving plants in full sun and expect them to grow," she said. "You have to work with what you have. We can't make our gardens into something they're not."

When I took her advice, my yard experienced a transformation. Zinnias bloomed where the impatiens had wilted, geraniums filled my window boxes, and lantana grew taller than my mailbox.

My life has experienced a similar transformation as I accept who I am and don't try to be someone I'm not. Instead of trying to be a social butterfly, I've learned to be content with a few good friends. While others paint, sing, and invent, I create word pictures. When my colleagues pursue high-profile positions, I embrace the ministry God has given me.

As I've learned to accept who God made me to be, I've blossomed almost as beautifully as my flower beds.

Father, thank You for making me just who
I need to be—for Your glory. Amen.
—Lori Hatcher

GROWING IN FAITH

What is one gift you have been given? Use it
today and thank God for making you just who *you* are.

ALL IN GOD'S TIMING

The law of the Lord *is perfect, refreshing the soul. The statutes of the* Lord *are trustworthy, making wise the simple.* —Psalm 19:7 (NIV)

We had lived next door to our neighbors for over a decade and they'd never planted a vegetable garden, so when they put one in last year, I watched with great interest. For several days in a row, the family of three worked until the ground was finally ready for the seeds to go into the earth. They were methodical, spacing the seeds several inches apart and labeling each row of vegetables. Sure enough, they had a harvest by mid-May. Surprisingly, after hauling in their leafy treasures, they started the process all over again.

What are they planting now? I wondered. *More peas? More onions? More broccoli?*

Finally, I asked them, learning that various vegetables have different growing seasons. In May, they planted corn; it would be ready for harvest in August.

Sitting in my writing chair, looking out the sunroom window, I watched that corn grow all summer and thought about how God has different growing seasons in our spiritual lives too. You see, if you plant a vegetable in the wrong growing season, it can die prematurely because the conditions are too harsh for it to even maintain dormancy. Or it can sprout but never thrive because the conditions aren't exactly right.

That's why we must wait patiently for God's perfect timing to bring our dreams to fruition. But we wait with joy, anticipating our next harvest.

Trust me; your harvest is coming!

Thank You, God, for You are trustworthy. Help me to wait patiently and with hopeful expectancy. Amen.

—Michelle Medlock Adams

GROWING IN FAITH

Trust God's perfect timing today.

MAINTENANCE MATTERS

I rise before dawn and cry for help; I have put my hope in your word.
—Psalm 119:147 (NIV)

One of the most challenging parts of gardening for me is the never-ending routine maintenance. This past July and August, our typical Texas heat was accompanied by unusually high humidity. About this same time, I couldn't work my garden due to illness. My lovely vegetables and flowers became an unruly mess.

Once I recovered and the humidity and heat died down, I went back to work, tackling one area of my garden at a time. Three months later, I was *still* trying to get all the deferred maintenance under control.

But I'm learning that's typical of life. Every endeavor needs routine grass cutting, which if ignored, creates mountains of work down the road. Sadly, sometimes my maintenance work is deferred, not for good reasons but because I choose to do something less important.

Nothing is more important than my relationship with the Lord. Yet how easy it is to let life dictate the terms rather than staying in step with His Spirit. When I succumb to the enemy's temptation to let spiritual matters slide, life becomes so much less than what God wants for me.

Thankfully, He is unchanging in His great love. He welcomes me back with open arms, helping me clean up each mountainous and unruly mess.

Oh God, forgive my often-wandering heart. Forgive me for neglecting my most prized possession, my relationship with You. Teach me, Lord, to quiet my heart daily to spend time with You, my greatest love. Amen.
—Cathy Bryant

GROWING IN FAITH

Like the Psalmist, cry out to the Lord through prayer today. Read His Word to find hope.

A RESTORATIVE ENDEAVOR

And the God of all grace, who called you to his eternal glory in Christ, after you have suffered a little while, will himself restore you and make you strong, firm and steadfast. —1 Peter 5:10 (NIV)

The Cameron Peak Fire, the largest recorded in Colorado history, burned within miles of our home. At night, the menacing orange glow of flames danced behind the foothills edging our neighborhood. On windy days, the fire raced toward town, devouring our favorite hiking trails. Entire ecosystems were destroyed. The fire burned for over three months.

Years later, my knees press into the mulch in our pollinator garden. The air is clear—something I no longer take for granted following the choking smoke during August that year. I sense not only the remedial benefits of tending to our plants, but I also feel a deeper connection. Our garden is full of plants native to this area—the very ones the flames claimed.

Every August is thrilling in the Rocky Mountains. Our meadows are aglow with wildflowers. This is one of my favorite seasons in the garden; now my efforts are part of a bigger picture of redemption. I watch firecracker penstemon and blue harebells unfurl from tight buds in our garden. Bees and butterflies stop over to sip nectar. Up the canyon, bright pink fireweed grows like a vibrant carpet across the once-charred forest floor.

God is inviting me into this restorative endeavor, and I get to take part in His work of making all things new.

Lord, I know that in the wake of hardship, You make all things new.

—Eryn Lynum

GROWING IN FAITH

Write down a difficult circumstance from the past year, then three ways God is growing you from that hardship.

All my hurts my garden spade can heal.

RALPH WALDO EMERSON,
POET AND PHILOSOPHER

GROWING PEACE

You are my hiding place; you will protect me from trouble and surround me with songs of deliverance. —Psalm 32:7 (NIV)

My husband has been working "across the pond" in Belgium all summer. I'm stressed. Our teenaged sons are easy, but the responsibility of maintaining a household is not. I traveled miles for one son's state swim meet and moved another home from college and then back again. I chauffeured a boy to clubs and classes that started with the rising sun. Appliances have gone on strike. There were two fender-benders. And I just miss my husband like wild.

The duration of separation is indefinite; my strength is not.

I walk to the back garden to gather vegetables for dinner. The beds are raised, so I sit on the ground. I reach for a red bell pepper, and it's warm from the sun. The tomatoes are too. They're full and ripe in my hand.

This garden is flourishing.

For the first time this evening, I notice the color of the sky. It's a wash of pastel. The sun is reaching with rays of late-day gold. And a breeze sings soprano on my wind chimes. The ground beneath me holds heat from the day, and when my Labrador sits beside me, I'm calmed. I think about how God placed Adam and Eve in a garden. It's where His provision runs rich. He provided all that was needed then, and He'll provide for me too.

I breathe deep.

Tension slips from my shoulders.

I'm hidden in holiness, protected and at peace in this place.

Lord, thank You for Your presence and provision.
You alone bring peace. Amen.
—Shawnelle Eliasen

GROWING IN FAITH

When stress hits hard today, look at your life and identify one way God is present and providing for you.

A HEAVENLY FRAGRANCE

You prepare a table before me in the presence of my enemies. You anoint my head with oil; my cup overflows. —Psalm 23:5 (NIV)

Amid my garden is a special place where I meditate, relax, and talk to God. Under the shelter are rocking chairs, hammocks with the perfect view of clouds, and a small table surrounded by gardenias, vinca vines, and hanging potted flowers.

One day, at the beginning of summer, I was looking forward to soaking up sun in one of the hammocks when I was startled by an invasion of spiders. Agitated by these unwelcome guests, I remembered that peppermint oil thwarts ants, mice, spiders, and other pests. So I purchased and transplanted several small peppermint plants into large ceramic pots as a defense around the shelter. After a week, the spiders permanently moved out.

Later, in the peak of summer, I was taking a nap in my hammock when a breeze stirred up a thick aroma of peppermint. I turned my attention to the nearest peppermint plant. Leaning toward it, I observed the mint was completely saturated, originating from the center of the plant, constantly dripping oil off the tip of each leaf.

I instantly felt the presence of God. The fragrance and precious oil imparted insight into how He wants me to operate. Like the leaves attached to the main plant, I am meant to ceaselessly abide in Jesus. As the Lord's habitation, He is my provision and reduces my enemies to onlookers. As a result, heavenly fragrance will constantly saturate my life and benefit those around me.

Jesus, I want to abide in You.

—Jessi Creed

GROWING IN FAITH

Stop worrying about difficult circumstances or people in your life. Rest at the table Jesus has prepared for you.

SOWING FREELY

Cast your bread upon the waters, for you will find it after many days.
—Ecclesiastes 11:1 (ESV)

Last spring, my husband bought a packet of assorted seeds labeled "Wildflowers." We cleared a spot around the edge of our peony bed and planted them, curious about what would later sprout and bloom.

Later in the summer, a huge variety of shapes and colors sprang up. Each time I sat outside, my gaze gravitated to those flowers, and they made me smile.

Gardeners sometimes take a risk and cast seeds without any guarantee of what will emerge. My life also has moments of casting out in faith. I might send a card to a friend, not knowing if the germ of support will take root and bloom into the encouragement she needs. I might spend years scattering words into a novel, not knowing if the story will land in the hearts of readers. As a parent, I sought to plant love and truth in the lives of my children and after "many days" have seen them blossom.

There are various interpretations of this proverb from Ecclesiastes, but I believe it's a lovely verse for gardeners.

We can sow generously and widely.

We can sow in many directions.

We can sow without fear.

Then we watch and wait as God brings our seeds to life!

Dear Lord, grant us faith to cast out seeds, trusting You for the results. Thank You for Your promise that after we sow, we will also reap. Amen.
—Sharon Hinck

GROWING IN FAITH

Has the Holy Spirit nudged you to sow a blessing in someone else's life? Take a risk today and cast out your service, thanking God for the results He will bring.

WHAT'S BUGGING YOU?

Teach me your way, Lord, that I may rely on your faithfulness.
—Psalm 86:11 (NIV)

One summer, I had a zucchini vine that sprouted and spread, covering more area than our garden bed could handle. As each yellow flower bloomed, one after the other, I imagined the zucchini casseroles, cakes, and breads that were surely in my future.

But no fruit ever came from the vast vine.

We eventually figured out that we had been overzealous with the insect repellent we sprayed in early spring. We had inadvertently removed all potential pollinators. It's difficult to wrap our brains around the fact that creepy, crawly bugs are important, even necessary. But the truth is, without these assumed annoyances our garden can't grow.

Isn't that the way we treat all pests and problems in our lives? They bother us, and we want them gone. Erased. We pray for relief and release.

Of course, there's nothing wrong with telling God what is in our heart. But God reminds us that everything is for a reason. All that He has placed in our lives has a purpose, even when we don't see it.

Instead of praying for our problems simply to be gone, perhaps we should also pray to discover what we need to learn from our perceived predicaments.

Only with that new understanding can our lives truly bear fruit.

God, when I am annoyed, bothered, or frightened by something in my life, remind me to look for the lesson You have intended for me. Help me to find peace in the problem while waiting on the solution.
—Tamara Bundy

GROWING IN FAITH

What is worrying you? What struggle are you going through? Ask God today what He might be teaching you through this.

I AM BLESSED

You shall eat the fruit of the labor of your hands; you shall be blessed, and it shall be well with you. —Psalm 128:2 (ESV)

I placed dinner for my husband, Zane, and me on the table. Almost everything was from my garden. The pasta was topped with Tie-Dye, yellow, and Sungold tomatoes and fresh basil. We also had a salad with purple kale, mixed greens, cherry tomatoes, and fresh thyme. I served homemade sourdough bread with rosemary-infused olive oil. It was rewarding to enjoy the fruit of my labor, but I felt like something was missing.

I missed our kids. I wished our adult sons were around to share this bounty with us. I expected, at this empty-nest stage of life, that a meal like this would be enjoyed by our family. Rather than experiencing the joy of this meal with my husband, I was entertaining a mental pity party. Then I saw Zane survey our food. He took a few bites. "Wow, this is amazing!" he said. "Everything tastes incredible." He knew how much time I had put into the garden that produced the food we were enjoying, and he let me know it.

Zane's words of encouragement lifted me out of self-pity. As Psalm 128:2 expresses, we were enjoying the fruit of my labor. Some other time, our boys will be with us, and someday I hope to see our family expand and fill the seats around the table.

But, for today, I am blessed, and all is well.

God, help me to enjoy the fruit of my labor and remember each day how You have blessed me. Amen.

—Jeannie Blackmer

GROWING IN FAITH

What is one blessing you are thankful for today? Tell or text someone about this good thing.

UPROOTING

The name of the Lord is a fortified tower; the righteous run to it and are safe. —Proverbs 18:10 (NIV)

The hydrangea plant was beautiful. Deep pink flowers amid rich dark leaves begged me to take it home, and I knew the perfect place where I'd plant it.

At home, I took care to dig the hole deep enough and amend the soil properly. Every day I checked the plant to see how it was doing, and I was disappointed to discover that, after a few weeks, the leaves lost their deep green color and turned brown on the edges, and the flowers that attempted to blossom wilted.

What was wrong? Was it getting enough water? Did I need to fertilize it?

No matter what I did, the plant wasn't flourishing. It looked worse each day. I decided to research the situation, as well as to observe the hydrangeas in other people's yards.

It wasn't long before I discovered the problem: the plant was getting too much sun. Too many hours in our hot summer sun was too much for this shade-loving plant. It needed to be moved.

What I had thought was the perfect place was wrong for that particular plant. I moved it to a more suitable place, and the plant thrived.

Several years ago, God uprooted me, moving me from an area where I was not experiencing growth to a new place where I have found new life.

And I am so thankful He did.

Lord, thank You for knowing just where we belong to live and thrive.

—Marilyn Turk

GROWING IN FAITH

Consider inviting a newcomer to your community for coffee or to an event where they can meet people and establish their roots.

BEAUTY IN AUGUST

This is what God the L*ORD* *says—the Creator of the heavens, who stretches them out, who spreads out the earth with all that springs from it, who gives breath to its people, and life to those who walk on it.* —Isaiah 42:5 (NIV)

"A purple passionflower!" My niece, Sophi, cupped the blossom on a twisting vine. As a regular on my field trips into nature and the daughter of my biologist brother, she possessed a keen eye for identifying flora even then, at the age of eleven.

"Oh, what a fun name," I said. "And the flower looks like something out of a cartoon!"

The curious bloom resembled a pile of flower parts, as if God had stacked layer upon playful layer to create a whimsical masterpiece. Five white sepals—the leaves under a bloom that support and protect it—lay under five lavender petals; they formed a symmetrical circle of ten. Above that, wavy strands covered the passionflower with purple "fringe." Finally, the upright stamens and stigmas adorned the center of the blossom, in fountain fashion, on the very top of it all.

God's garden is animated—lively and inspiring—brushed with shades of purple and trimmed in floral frills. God could have placed us in a simple creation, with bland hues and quiet views. But He didn't. Instead, He spread out purple passionflowers for us to enjoy, along with other marvels of nature that spring from the earth.

Dear Masterful Maker, Your floral designs captivate us.
Thank You for the beauty we find in each bloom!
—Becky Alexander

GROWING IN FAITH

Sketch a flower that blooms in August where you live. Thank God for adding detail and color to the plant and for placing you in His lively garden.

UNWELCOME GUESTS

We demolish arguments and every pretension that sets itself up against the knowledge of God, and we take captive every thought to make it obedient to Christ. —2 Corinthians 10:5 (NIV)

My thirteen-year-old son, Isaiah, and I worked hard in our garden. We'd started the plants from seeds and rejoiced when skinny, spindly tomato plants, stems thin as threads, grew thick and hearty and strong. Later, yellow blossoms brought us joy. The plants grew tall and wide fast, making surrounding them with cylinder cages a challenge. But when the tomatoes grew, first tiny and green, then into great, glorious globes gone red by the sun, our satisfaction was deep.

Then the bugs arrived. Small and white, looking like miniature fairies, they were destructive.

"Mom, the plants are dying," Isaiah said. His green eyes were sorrowful. We had dreams of BLTs. We had aspirations of salsa-making.

"Let's help them!" I said.

We tried vinegar washes and diatomaceous earth, a powder that dehydrates and then kills insects. We clipped bottom branches. But the bugs stayed, and the plants withered.

"They're trying, Mom," Isaiah said. "But these plants are weak."

Standing there with loss swelling tight in my chest, I saw a spiritual correlation. Recently I'd been struggling with negative thoughts. I'd been criticizing and judging others and myself. These thoughts were destructive, like the fluffy, white pests that gnawed at our healthy tomato plants. Wrong thinking damages the spirit, and fruitfulness takes a hit.

"Do you think there's any hope?" my son asked.

I wasn't sure about the plants. But hope for my thought-life? Yes!

I knew where to go: Jesus would bring hope and health.

Lord, show me when my thoughts are unhealthy. Amen.

—Shawnelle Eliasen

GROWING IN FAITH

Today fight the battle of the mind by taking negative thought-guests to Jesus.

WAITING AND WORRYING

Be joyful in hope, patient in affliction, faithful in prayer.
—Romans 12:12 (NIV)

Once, after a season of having grown fantastic sunflowers, I harvested and dried their seeds before putting them in an airtight container. And, miracles of all miracles, I remembered where this container was when it was time to plant them in pots a few weeks before the last frost.

Each of my four children planted some seeds in a pot of their own.

Then we waited.

Within days, little buds began to peek out, and my kids were thrilled.

Truthfully, everyone was thrilled except my youngest. His seeds weren't growing yet. However, he was growing... impatient. He didn't understand. *Why did he have to wait? Was there something wrong with his seeds? His pot? Him?*

Isn't this like our prayer life?

When we have to wait for answers, we grow impatient. This frustration is made worse when we suspect others' prayers are being answered when it feels as though ours are not heard at all.

My son's sunflower was growing beneath the surface long before he could see the results. In fact, he would end up proud that his grew the tallest of *all* the flowers that year.

Just like a plant that seems it will never grow, we need to remember that God is always answering us, even if we are unable to see a simple sprout of an answer just yet.

God, help me to find the blend of persistence and patience in my prayer life. Enable me to fully trust in You even when I can't immediately see how You are answering me.
—Tamara Bundy

GROWING IN FAITH

Spend a few minutes reflecting on a way God answered one of your prayers. Was the timing what you hoped for? The result?

PROTECTING THE PRODUCE

But the fruit of the Spirit is love, joy, peace, forbearance, kindness, goodness, faithfulness, gentleness and self-control. Against such things there is no law. —Galatians 5:22–23 (NIV)

Have you seen the movie *Field of Dreams*? It has the iconic line: "If you build it, they will come."

As a gardener, I swap out the word "build" with "plant."

"If you *plant* it, they will come." And by "they," I mean the deer and other critters who live in my area. Just about anything I plant becomes a snack for them. To protect my garden, I maintain a sturdy fence to keep the wildlife out.

Boundaries serve two purposes. They keep unwanted things out as well as protect what is inside. The Bible is the inspired Word of God and sets the boundaries for living the godly life. Applying it protects me from outside threats and keeps the things I produce unharmed. I can produce the fruit of the Spirit if I use the Word of God to ward off things aimed at destroying my spiritual garden.

Protecting my crops from predators gains me a harvest. When I protect my spiritual garden with the guidelines found within Scripture, God gains a spiritual harvest that can be shared with others.

A harvest like love, joy, peace, kindness, and faithfulness.

Father God, thank You for those seed savers and planters that You sowed into my soul at the right time. Thank You also for sending others to water and tend to my development. May the fruit produced in me yield seeds of faith that I will sow into others. Amen.

—Ben Cooper

GROWING IN FAITH

Spend time today in God's Word.
Ask Him to sow new seeds of faith in you.

CLIMB OF THE CLEMATIS

Awake, north wind, and come, south wind! Blow on my garden, that its fragrance may spread everywhere. —Song of Songs 4:16 (NIV)

A brilliant blue sky is the perfect backdrop for the deep royal purple clematis that stretches up the iron trellis. I have waited and watched in anticipation every day to see her come to life again.

The trellis, built for the weight of her heavy vines and blossoms, sits just inside the garden gate, with clematis planted on each side.

It is an amazing transformation every spring to watch the tender vines come to life, inching their way upward until they finally make contact with the trellis. Once they find it—sometimes with my help—they grow and climb very quickly. In fact, I think if I were to stand and watch them, it may be possible to *see* them growing.

Every visit to my garden is an adventure and true example of God's creation. There is such wonder and peace in these moments, in these quiet miracles.

The ladies of the garden, the clematis hostess to them all—the hollyhocks in their colorful gauze skirts; the pansies with their bright, expressive faces; the lily of the valley churning her own spectacular, blustery fragrance—are treasures, all made by the Lord God.

Like the flowers, I feel clothed with strength, dignity, and perseverance, knowing that only God can make things grow. Our own climb to victory is just as amazing as those in the garden. I sow wildflower seeds there and encourage all to grow wildly. I have planted seeds of hope there.

Heavenly Father, thank You for all that You provide—beauty, fragrance, faith, and grace.
—Cookie Cranston

GROWING IN FAITH

Today spend a few minutes reflecting on the beauty God has planted in you.

CHOKED OUT

Other seed fell among thorns, which grew up and choked the plants, so that they did not bear grain... Others, like seed sown among thorns, hear the word; but the worries of this life, the deceitfulness of wealth and the desires for other things come in and choke the word, making it unfruitful.
—Mark 4:7, 18–19 (NIV)

I used to have a bountiful strawberry bed with an equally thriving row of raspberries behind it. About the time the strawberries peaked in production, the raspberries would begin to ripen, so our summers were blessed with bowls of fresh fruit and our winters blessed with jam we'd made with excess fruit.

However, we developed a problem. The raspberries spread, continually shooting up new canes in the middle of the strawberries, and when I went to pull them, the abundance of thorns pierced through my garden gloves. The remaining canes grew even taller, then once loaded with ripening fruit, bent low under the weight, casting shade over the strawberries. The result was just like Jesus's parable of the seed among the thorns—only a few strawberry plants survived, and none produced a single fruit.

It's possible to live a fruitful life alongside the occasional worry, pursuit of financial goals, and desire for the latest gadget. Possible, yes. But chances are that unless I'm diligent to cultivate the fruitful areas of my life while simultaneously limiting others, materialism could multiply like thorny bushes, choking out spiritual growth.

Like my backyard example, I must know when to cut back the intruders so fruit can grow again.

Jesus, forgive me for allowing materialism to choke out the work You are doing in my life.
—Candee Fick

GROWING IN FAITH

Today just say no to that next purchase, online order, or shopping trip and instead meditate on God's goodness and provision.

The making of a garden is much like the formation of character—the loveliest mature characters are often the result of many early mistakes.

HANNA RION VERBECK,
PAINTER, MUSICIAN, AND WRITER

FRUITS OF FRIENDSHIP

How abundant are the good things that you have stored up for those who fear you, that you bestow in the sight of all, on those who take refuge in you. —Psalm 31:19 (NIV)

"The birdbath is perfect," Susan said. "I'll fill it with marbles and water for the bees in my garden."

She smiled the dimpled smile I remembered from high school. We were just acquaintances then, although I'd prayed we'd become friends. I admired Susan's straightforward but kind demeanor. Now, thirty years later, we reunited after she'd answered my Facebook Marketplace ad.

"Would you like to come in for tea?" I asked.

Susan did, and conversation was easy. Two hours later, I felt sad as we hugged goodbye. I was still drawn to Susan, but life was busy. I didn't expect to see her again—until she posted an ad for free tomatoes.

"I'd love some!" I typed. A bug invasion had withered and wasted my own plants. "Share your address? I'll come by tomorrow."

The next day, we stood on Susan's drive as she handed me a basket brimming with beautiful tomatoes. We talked for an hour.

"I'll have more tomatoes next week," she said when I needed to head home. "I'll be in touch."

But when she texted, I was down with a migraine.

"I'm sorry," I typed. "A headache won't let me pick the tomatoes up. Please share with someone else."

Susan's response made my soul smile.

"I'll deliver!" she typed. "But what else can I do for you? I want to help."

I felt better already.

God had used our gardens to grow fruits of friendship.

Lord, give me eyes to see Your unexpected gifts. Amen.
—Shawnelle Eliasen

GROWING IN FAITH

Thank the Lord for unexpected gifts.

EASY OR CHALLENGING

"Don't look for shortcuts to God. The market is flooded with surefire, easygoing formulas for a successful life that can be practiced in your spare time. Don't fall for that stuff, even though crowds of people do. The way to life—to God!—is vigorous and requires total attention."

—Matthew 7:13–14 (MSG)

Friends who stop by in the late summer get the same offer from me: "Would you like some zucchini?"

I don't even like zucchini much, so why do I keep growing it, then desperately find myself needing to give it away? Because it's easy! The squirrels that decimate my tomatoes leave the zucchini alone. The deer that eat peppers and beans ignore it.

I often take that approach to living my faith. I spend time on easy pursuits that don't stretch my trust in God. Taking the safe route, I'm guaranteed *some* produce.

But when I follow Christ on a more challenging path—when I take up my cross and follow Him in forgiving someone who hurts me, in making a call to a friend even when I'm feeling shy, or in accepting a new writing project or a speaking engagement that scares me—the results He produces are worth it.

I draw so much pleasure in my garden from the more difficult plants: the finicky rose that finally blooms, the new potatoes that melt in my mouth, and the pumpkin that requires a lot of room. They aren't always the easiest, but why settle for easy?

Dear Lord, thank You for helping us trust You instead of defaulting to the easiest choices.

—Sharon Hinck

GROWING IN FAITH

What is one risk you can take today that you feel God has been nudging you toward? Step forward in faith, knowing He will be with you.

THE GLORY OF A MORNING GLORY

The LORD has done this, and it is marvelous in our eyes.
—Psalm 118:23 (NIV)

The odd leaf caught my eye when I passed by the chain-link fence. It blended in with the thick foliage of a red coral honeysuckle. Several years ago, the honeysuckle had planted itself in this corner flower bed and now draped over the fence.

What now grew entangled within the honeysuckle? I stopped to examine the five-lobed leaf. Then I found an unfurled blossom, long and lavender. A morning glory, I concluded. I couldn't wait for the flower to open.

In the meantime, I pondered the mysterious vine. Could it be tievine, a morning glory that grew on its own in our native plant gardens? No, the leaves weren't the same. Or Alamo vine, a native I'd planted by seed farther down the fence? Again, the leaves differed.

That left Lindheimer's morning glory. But the native vine didn't grow in our neighborhood. Next, I checked my blog. According to a post, eight years ago I'd planted three Lindheimer's morning glories in the same area. But they must have died without blooming. The loss had saddened me. *But now could one have returned? All these years later? Another of Your mysterious ways, Lord?*

Two days later, the lavender bloom opened, revealing a white center. Bingo! The vine *was* a Lindheimer's morning glory. *How could that have happened?* I'll never know for sure. But God does. In His honor, I give Him all the glory.

And so do all my morning glories.

Lord, thank You for the marvelous miracles
I've witnessed in the garden. Amen.
—Sheryl Smith-Rodgers

GROWING IN FAITH

Look with fresh eyes at your garden. Reflect on what has surprised you or has come back when you thought it had died.

CONSULTING WITH THE PRO

Listen to counsel and receive instruction, That you may be wise in your latter days. —Proverbs 19:20 (NKJV)

Challenging myself to go outside my comfort zone this season, I planted seeds for flowers I'd never grown before. Only one took root from the entire packet. At every stage of growth, I kept questioning why it looked so odd. I had to keep reminding myself that it was a new plant for me.

I did eventually realize it was a weed. However, by then it had grown so tall and strong, it took all my might to uproot it. Worse yet, burrs stuck to my clothes when I disposed of it in the woods. Had I consulted a gardening pro early on, she would have identified it as a weed and advised me to pull it immediately.

I've had similar experiences in the garden of my life. I've taken on things that were unfamiliar to me. Despite the nagging feeling that something wasn't quite right, I've continued on, allowing some negative things to take root and grow in my life. Later, when I finally saw things for what they were, it was always more difficult to extricate myself. Inevitably, there was residual fallout that clung to me like those burrs on my clothes.

I need to remember that when something doesn't sit right, it's a prompt to consult with Jesus. He's the pro in every circumstance. He'll either support me through the new experience or identify when it's not right for me, prompting me to uproot it from my life.

Wise Counselor, remind me to seek Your wisdom in all I do. Amen.

—Claire McGarry

GROWING IN FAITH

Inspect your garden today. If anything looks unfamiliar or could be a problem, consult an expert for advice.

FAITHFUL HARVEST

I will consider all your works and meditate on all your mighty deeds.
—Psalm 77:12 (NIV)

I snapped string beans at my parents' table. Old enamel canners bubbled steam on the stove. The air was sweet with scent: it was canning day.

Dad set a box of jars on the floor. Most were clear and clean, but one jar held spiced green beans.

"The beans were hiding behind the empties," he said. "They're six years old!"

He handed me the jar and said, "Take these to my grandson."

My husband and I have five sons, but I knew which one Dad meant. I counted back six years, and that one had been a tough year for our teen. Hard things had happened. There had been heartache. Shared time around the table had been rare. Yet I remembered canning day that year. Our son had joined us as we trimmed beans and sliced garlic. He'd loved the beans and had eaten them fast and fresh while we packed the jars.

I now held the cool jar in my hand and thought of him.

Miracles had happened. He was healthy. Our relationship had healed and was growing. The work of the Lord had been powerful. His goodness showered land that had been barren. The harvest of blessing was rich and sweet.

"Six years was a long time ago," I said.

Dad nodded and rested his hand on my shoulder.

If we ever doubt the presence of God, we need only look to where He has been.

Lord, Your goodness of old gives me hope anew. Amen.
—Shawnelle Eliasen

GROWING IN FAITH

Today when you become discouraged,
remember the Lord's goodness in the past.

HAPPY WORK

Moreover, when God gives someone wealth and possessions, and the ability to enjoy them, to accept their lot and be happy in their toil—this is a gift of God. —Ecclesiastes 5:19 (NIV)

I find gardening to be extremely satisfying work. There is just something about dirt under my fingernails that feels good. When I garden, I can easily see the fruits of my labor. The orderly rows of fresh flowers after planting. The cleaned-up beds after weeding. And harvesting tomatoes is one of the most satisfying things in the world to me.

Things don't work as neatly in my day job as a pastor. I can prepare and preach what I hope is a wonderful sermon, but I am not sure any wisdom or faith will grow in the hearts of my parishioners. I can come alongside someone in moments of hardship or tragedy, but I can't know how much difference I've made. It's not as easy to see and enjoy the fruits of my labor at the church as it is in the garden.

The poet of Ecclesiastes reminds us that to be happy in our work is a gift from God. The truth is, I love my pastoral ministry. And my faith tells me that to be able to do a job I love is nothing short of a gift.

But gardening is another kind of blessing. An orderly spring bed, a freshly weeded summer patch, and a sun-ripened tomato are all gifts that bring me joy.

And that joy sustains me in my regular job as well.

Thank You, God, for the order and beauty I find in nature.

—Heather Jepsen

GROWING IN FAITH

Think about a task that feels satisfying for you. Thank God for the joy it brings.

GLORIOUS AND GLOWING FROM WITHIN

The Lord is not slow to fulfill his promise as some count slowness.
—2 Peter 3:9 (ESV)

Every other flower I tend seems to be eager to make its presence known, all but my morning glories. They poke along, indistinguishable from the weed seedlings that are just getting their start too. The tiny tendrils eventually find purchase on the stakes I've planted for them. But trip after trip to the garden shows peonies having a riotous time. Geraniums and marigolds in hanging baskets almost luminesce in their desire to be seen. Even chive flowers wave their lavender flower explosions on thin tall stems.

But I find nothing but vines where morning glory blossoms should be. Day after day. Plenty of green but no blooms. Lovely and delicate. But the longed-for blossoms seem so slow in coming.

Then... ah! "There you are, little one!" A blossom unfurls in that spiral way morning glories own. Face to the sun. Glowing within. Every year, when I think this is the year they'll fail to come at all, they surprise and delight me.

And so do God's answers to my prayers. They rarely arrive on my timetable. They sometimes hide behind what I assume are crises. They don't announce themselves with fanfare. But there they are. Glorious and glowing from within. Bringing joy and reminding me that it is impossible for God to fail, no matter how long I've been waiting.

God, forgive me for moments of doubt. Help me to trust
Your timing as well as Your faithfulness.
—Cynthia Ruchti

GROWING IN FAITH

Do you keep a prayer journal? Not just a list of prayer needs, but an ongoing record of requests and answered prayers? Our doubts often flee when we can trace a pattern of answers. Consider starting one today.

PREPARED BY GOD

For we are God's handiwork, created in Christ Jesus to do good works, which God prepared in advance for us to do. —Ephesians 2:10 (NIV)

There comes a time in every gardening season when I find myself at a standstill, feeling a sense of utter awe. This past year was no exception.

One day, it dawned on me that surrounding me were the plants I started inside as seeds or sowed directly into the ground—and even some I hadn't planted at all. Those volunteer plants were a gift from God. Although they left my garden looking like an unruly jungle, they also added a layer of beauty that could only be attributed to the Master Gardener.

God works similarly in our lives.

Though the term *master gardener* is a title many gardeners strive to earn, the Lord is truly the one and only Master Gardener. While He is unequaled in growing gardens, He also does magnificent work in human hearts.

Sometimes I balk at what life holds in store for me, but God uses even difficulty to mold masterpieces, which in turn produce a crop of good deeds that He prepared ahead of time for me to accomplish.

Once more, I stand in awe, not at my temporary garden, but at His amazing plan for His people.

Lord God, there is no one like You. No one can do what You do. You created me and You're making me over into a masterpiece to carry on Your work and Your perfect plan. I stand in awe of You. Amen.

—Cathy Bryant

GROWING IN FAITH

Set aside a few minutes to prayerfully consider what good works the Master Gardener might have for you to do. Take one small step today to complete one of them.

Everything that slows us down and forces patience, everything that sets us back into the slow circles of nature, is a help. Gardening is an instrument of grace.

MAY SARTON, WRITER

IN THE COOL OF THE DAY

Then the man and his wife heard the sound of the Lord *God as he was walking in the garden in the cool of the day.*—Genesis 3:8 (NIV)

When was the "cool of the day" when Adam and Eve walked with God?

Most will say it was the morning. The familiar hymn "In the Garden," written by C. Austin Miles, suggests the cool of the day was while the plants were dripping wet with moisture from the dew. Others might claim it was the evening. A third possible answer often gets overlooked: it could have been both. All we know for sure is that it wasn't at noon when temperatures are normally highest.

I choose to believe it was *both* morning and evening.

One common theme in the Scriptures is God's desire to have a relationship with us. We should not limit the timing or how often fellowship took place between the Creator and Adam and Eve in the Garden of Eden.

Have you ever envisioned what the garden God planted looked like? Imagine strolling with God against a backdrop of every beneficial plant in existence, knowing that when He planted it, He said it was good. Think of the nourishment Adam and Eve received fellowshipping with God.

Walking with Him each morning and evening would be the perfect way to spend the day. And we can choose to do that too!

Lord God, thank You for wanting a relationship with me. Please give me a desire to begin and end each day by being refreshed through prayer and Bible reading, as I spend time with You. Amen.

—Ben Cooper

GROWING IN FAITH

Today schedule a block of time to enjoy a refreshing "cool of the day" with the Lord.

TASTE AND SEE

Oh, taste and see that the Lord is good; Blessed is the man who trusts in Him! —Psalm 34:8 (NKJV)

This year, I planted a cabbage plant. I don't remember ever eating cabbage before, other than sauerkraut, but I thought it was a unique vegetable, so decided to try growing it. As the summer progressed, big green leaves flourished, but the cabbage plant didn't seem to be producing anything edible. Frustrated, I gave up on it. Then, near the end of summer, seemingly out of nowhere, a little tight ball in the middle of the giant leaves appeared. The cabbage grew quickly. It was a beautiful vegetable; I even took photos of it. When it was a decent size, I plucked it, sliced it, and sautéed it in olive oil, thyme, salt, and pepper. It was good—in fact it was delicious!

In Psalm 34, God invites us to taste and see that He is good. I love that He created us with our senses, and He reveals Himself to us through them. As a new gardener, I've noticed an awareness of my senses has been heightened, and I've gotten to enjoy God in a fresh, tangible way. I see the beauty of His creation in the details of a cabbage plant. I touch the earth and feel His provision. I taste His goodness in the vegetables I grow and eat. I smell His pleasant fragrance in my roses. I hear His voice in songs of the birds. I get to experience Him in new ways and am continually assured He is good.

Dear Father, let me taste and see Your goodness today.
—Jeannie Blackmer

GROWING IN FAITH

Pay attention to how you experience God through one of your senses today, then journal about it.

MAMA'S LILIES

For we live by faith, not by sight. —2 Corinthians 5:7 (NIV)

A fierce orange they were. We called them tiger lilies; they had speckles, stripes, and stamen that resembled the prominent whiskers of a tiger. I recall a showy border of them around my grandmother's home. The spiky green blades of foliage served as an attractive contrast to the long-stemmed blossoms emerging and pushing upward, stretching for God's sunshine.

The lilies are new to my yard but old in terms of their existence. They previously had been transplanted from my grandmother's home to my mother's home, and now they have landed in a treasured spot of God's real estate in my own garden.

Excited to have the lilies with us now, I waited with great anticipation for them to bloom. I nervously watched the black earth in springtime to show miracle-of-life evidence poking up from where the bulbs had been planted in the fall.

I feared that they had been transplanted one too many times and that they were fragile now as they aged, once again finding themselves in an unfamiliar situation. Yet I had faith that they would emerge and survive.

Like the lilies, I sometimes find myself on unfamiliar ground, needing to readjust and establish new roots to grow and bloom again. And like the lilies, I'm challenged to mirror their fiery reflective glow of strength, to be a brilliant light for others seeking the same in their own growing season.

Thank You, Father, for providing the gift of hope
from the soil and for nurturing our spiritual growth
while deepening the roots of our faith. Amen.
—Cookie Cranston

GROWING IN FAITH

Today, think about times in your life when God has transplanted you. Can you now discern why He wanted you in a new spot?

THE INDIAN HAWTHORNS

He cuts off every branch in me that bears no fruit, while every branch that does bear fruit he prunes so that it will be even more fruitful.
—John 15:2 (NIV)

I surveyed my flower beds that evening. A brutal ice storm last October and unprecedented snowfall with freezing temperatures in February made it one of the fiercest winters in Oklahoma history. It wreaked havoc on trees. Limbs were stacked high, awaiting pickup at the curbs of houses around town for months. Besides many broken tree branches, my Indian hawthorns were stringy and ragged. Once two feet across, the wood was now dead. There was nothing to do but cut them way back and pray they'd make it.

The slow-growing shrubs were ugly all summer. I considered digging them up several times, but by September, I noticed something remarkable. My Indian hawthorns' leaves had filled in. Not two feet across as they once were but fuller and more beautiful than ever after the severe cutting back I'd given them.

The symbolism was not lost on me. I'd faced unprecedented crises too—the end of a career, loss of loved ones, a friend's betrayal. Each situation left me feeling lifeless and alone, as barren and dead as my Indian hawthorns.

Looking at their leafy bows sparked hope in me. By trusting my Heavenly Gardener to prune me where needed, I'd develop resilience and spiritual fortitude to survive my own cruel winter and grow stronger and more beautiful in Him.

Creator God, please prune each nonproducing branch of my life. Amen.
—Stephanie Thompson

GROWING IN FAITH

Imagine the parts of your life as the branches of a shrub. Today identify what needs to be pruned to allow for growth.

THE HOURGLASS CUCUMBER

Do not conform to the pattern of this world, but be transformed by the renewing of your mind. Then you will be able to test and approve what God's will is—his good, pleasing and perfect will. —Romans 12:2 (NIV)

Grabbing my wooden gardening basket, I headed out to the garden to check if any cucumbers were ready to be picked. I was eager to make a batch of my mother-in-law's refrigerator pickles.

The cucumbers had decided to vine up the side of the fence, meaning I didn't need to bend over to harvest them. I walked down the fence row until my basket was nearly full when I noticed an oddly shaped cucumber. I pulled at it, but it wouldn't budge. Moving aside a leaf that had been blocking my view, I discovered the cucumber had grown in between the fence's chain links and had grown into an hourglass shape—fat at both ends and skinny in the middle. I tugged and tugged, but it was stuck. I had to break it in two to harvest it.

The pieces in my hands reminded me of the funny-looking vegetables displayed at my local produce stand. Peculiarly shaped squash revealed how they had grown to fit the mold of the pots they had been planted in.

I wondered: *Am I shaped by my environment, or am I being molded into the image of Christ?*

After I brought my harvest into the house, I opened my Bible to read more about the God *I* want to look like.

Jesus, transform my mind with Your Word, and form me into Your image so that I am beautiful in Your sight and an effective witness to the world.

—Beth Gormong

GROWING IN FAITH

Talk to Jesus now, asking Him to form your words and actions into His image today.

THE ROOT OF THE TRUTH

Then we... won't be tossed and blown about by every wind of new teaching. We will not be influenced when people try to trick us with lies so clever they sound like the truth. —Ephesians 4:14 (NLT)

My back protested as I tugged at the weed. When it pulled away from the ground, leaving the root still in the dirt, I gave it the stink eye. Weeding is no one's favorite task. I raise my hand high and straighten my achy back to that truth.

Weeds can choke a garden from the inside, or they can breach a garden's boundaries.

Weeds can crop up in our lives too. At times I have felt choked by bad attitudes that I needed to root out of my life. Other times I have recognized weeds of unhealthy connections and needed to restructure boundaries to maintain emotional, relational, and spiritual health.

It's easy to feel tangled up by weeds of other people's opinions and viewpoints. Some arguments can be very convincing, to the point that they create confusion and muddle our clarity. Getting to the root of truth can feel frustrating, like digging weeds out of rocky soil.

I love that God ably and patiently weeds our lives. In His capable hands, we can keep our interior and exterior boundaries in place, bloom in healthy ways, and live in His truth.

Lord, thank You for weeding out lies and misconceptions that can steer me wrong. Please tend to any weeds beginning to take root in my heart. Amen.

—Erin Keeley Marshall

GROWING IN FAITH

Do a weed check in your yard and heart this week.
Pray as you work and thank God for giving you clarity.

ANTS ON ROSES

"Watch and pray so that you will not fall into temptation. The spirit is willing, but the flesh is weak." —Matthew 26:41 (NIV)

A new bloom caught my eye. I approached my rosebush to admire its beauty and get a sniff of its sweet fragrance. A closer inspection, however, revealed hundreds of tiny ants crawling along the cane.

Why were ants on my roses? I looked it up and discovered they feed on the residue left on plants by aphids. I needed to remove the aphids to get rid of the ants.

I hosed down the roses to wash away the sticky substance left by the aphids. Then I sprinkled the grounds from my morning coffee around the base of the cane. An article said that coffee confuses the ants and causes them to lose their scent trails. I poured the used grounds around the bases of the bushes every day for a week. Finally, there were no more ants on my roses.

To get rid of the ants, I needed to get rid of what attracted them to my plants. That's true of my life as well. Blocking temptations, like spending too much time online or eating too many cookies or mindlessly scrolling on my phone, allows me to flourish. By setting limits on screen time or by leaving junk food at the store, I can be more like the person God wants me to be and bloom!

Jesus, thank You for being my strength when I am weak. By Your grace, help me to choose Your best for me. Amen.

—Crystal Storms

GROWING IN FAITH

Think of an area of temptation for you, then ask God what safeguard you can put in place to help you make a better choice.

OVERCOMPENSATING

Trust in the L*ORD with all your heart and lean not on your own understanding.* —Proverbs 3:5 (NIV)

For the first time in years, I decided to plant some flowers from seed. Out of nowhere, doubt crept in that maybe I didn't have a green thumb anymore. To compensate, I quadrupled the packets of seeds I used, figuring it would increase my odds of success. Oh my! You should have seen the excess of white alyssum that grew. What was supposed to be a dainty, low border encircling the garden turned into a jungle of gangly green stems with white clusters that blocked out the sunlight for the other plants. I should have followed the instructions on the packet and trusted nature and the process.

How often do I do the same thing in other areas of life? I volunteer for something that seems to be right for my skill set, and then doubt creeps in: *Can I really pull this off? Am I going to fall flat on my face and embarrass myself?* So I overcompensate and throw myself into the project 200 percent. Before you know it, it takes over my life. My other responsibilities get overshadowed and forgotten, and they're denied the attention and work they require. Worse yet, I lean on my own strength and ability rather than leaning into Jesus for the wisdom, confidence, and balance I need. I learn all over again that I should have followed His instructions in Proverbs 3 and trusted Him and His process.

Faithful Father, increase my trust so I lean into You in all things. Amen.

—Claire McGarry

GROWING IN FAITH

Write Proverbs 3:5 on an index card or in a note on your phone as a reminder to lean on Jesus, not on your own understanding.

CREATED ORDER

But God made the earth by his power; he founded the world by his wisdom and stretched out the heavens by his understanding.
—Jeremiah 10:12 (NIV)

Not long after my husband and I bought our first home, we planted a garden. We had no idea what we were doing and made plenty of mistakes. We planted a little of everything and watched to see what would come up.

One rookie mistake we made was planting our zucchini and pumpkins together. Imagine our surprise that fall to discover that we had a whole crop of zucchini-pumpkins on our hands. We didn't know anything about cross-pollination, but that summer we got our lesson when bees visited both the zucchini and the pumpkin flowers, mixing the plants up. When it came time for harvest, our zucchini looked fine, but they smelled and tasted like pumpkin. And, of all things, our mature pumpkins were totally green! We laughed so hard.

It can be easy for us to overlook the small wonders of God's creation. In the beginning, God created an ordered world. And part of that was plants and trees each bearing seed according to its kind. No cross-pollination there!

Life can be such a mess sometimes. And gardening is a messy business for sure. It is good to know that God creates order out of chaos and that all things are created according to their kinds.

I don't think God intended for us to grow zucchini-pumpkins, but the laughter my husband and I shared that fall brought us great joy.

"And God saw that it was good" (Genesis 1:18).

God, thank You for creating order from chaos. Amen.
—Heather Jepsen

GROWING IN FAITH

What gardening mistakes have given you an appreciation for God's created order? Reflect on them today.

ENRICHING OUR SOIL

Sow your seed in the morning, and at evening let your hands not be idle, for you do not know which will succeed, whether this or that, or whether both will do equally well. —Ecclesiastes 11:6 (NIV)

A few years ago, my husband and I bought a tumbler composter. We throw kitchen scraps, grass clippings, and shredded leaves into it, and we turn it frequently. We feed our garden beds with all the rich nutrients—compost nourishes all plants. And gardeners know the value of good soil.

Lately, the soil of my heart has felt like the hard clay under the surface in our backyard. I'm weary of the noise of the world, saddened by losses, and worried about things I can't control. I've curled in on myself, resisting the gentle tilling of my Gardener.

This week, due to health issues, we attended church online. It was easy for my mind to wander, to watch without singing along in the worship or reciting the creed with the congregation. But as I listened, sang, and prayed with the family of faith, the soil of my soul was loosened, and those spiritual nutrients were stirred in.

I long for God to produce a crop for His Kingdom out of my life. I can't expect my vegetables to produce if their soil isn't fed. I can't expect myself to bear a crop if I don't receive His nourishment.

What a gift that He provides ample ways to enrich the soil of our hearts!

Lord, thank You for the many ways You nourish our souls. Help us embrace those opportunities to pray, dive into Scripture, and worship. Amen.

—Sharon Hinck

GROWING IN FAITH

Feed the soil of your heart in a new way today.
Spend extra time in prayer, Bible reading, or worship.

Gardening takes a plot of land, a hoe, and willing muscles. Scratching the soil, harvesting garden fruits, are peaceful results. With a garden, there is hope.

GRACE FIRTH, WRITER

SOURCE OF LOVE

Then God said, "I give you every seed-bearing plant on the face of the whole earth and every tree that has fruit with seed in it. They will be yours for food." —Genesis 1:29 (NIV)

"Here it is!" my husband announced. "The very last tomato!"

In our house, we have a tradition: the last tomato of the season is used to make the perfect sandwich—a just-picked, beautifully ripe garden tomato on toasted white bread with a hint of mayonnaise and a dash of salt and pepper.

I prepared the sandwich, sliced it in half to share with my husband, and we sat on the front porch, savoring every bite.

"The end of summer," my husband said.

"Goes out with a yum," I answered.

Of everything we grow, tomatoes are my favorites. A vine-ripe tomato is a delectable treat, a gift, a blessing you literally can't buy at the grocery store.

As we shared our last tomato sandwich of summer, I thought of all the work that went into our garden and growing that fruit. We ordered the seeds, started seedlings indoors, watered, fought off slugs and other pests, buried the stems, mulched—it was a labor of love.

But, I reflected, none of our efforts would matter or be possible if not for the source of love, the One who makes the seeds, our living God.

Dear Creator God, thank You for the gifts of summer.

—Sabra Ciancanelli

GROWING IN FAITH

What is your favorite summer recipe?
Share it with a friend. Consider including a favorite verse from Scripture with the recipe too.

THE VINE IN MY NEIGHBOR'S YARD

Do not speak evil against one another… who are you that you judge your neighbor? —James 4:11–12 (RSV)

With every passing day, the bright green vine in my neighbor's front yard grew longer and leafier. Her property was already an eyesore. Many of the neighbors thought so, and we seldom hesitated to complain to each other about it. Her grass was always too high. Her shrubs were so out of control that they covered the windows. Worst of all, her yard was completely devoid of flowers. Could she not even bother to plant marigolds next to her mailbox post?

Now this giant ugly vine had crept from beside her porch steps almost to the street. Why hadn't she pulled it up when it first got started? Why didn't she take a sharp hoe to it before it metastasized even further?

Late one autumn afternoon, while strolling around the block, I noticed something round and orange in my neighbor's yard. At first, I thought it was a basketball. Wrong. It was a pumpkin—the most perfect pumpkin, in fact, that I'd ever seen. As I ventured into the yard to take a closer look, her front door opened, and she stepped onto the porch.

"Hi, neighbor," she said, smiling and pointing to the pumpkin. "Isn't it wonderful!"

Wordlessly, I nodded.

"I tossed my jack-o'-lantern off the porch rail and into the grass last fall and here's my reward," she said, eyes shining. "I'll be happy to save you some seeds from this one."

"Thank you," I replied. "That would be lovely."

I'm too quick to judge, Lord. Forgive me and help me to do better. Amen.

—Jennie Ivey

GROWING IN FAITH

Look for a way to appreciate someone you have judged in the past, rather than finding fault in them.

BEAUTY FOR ASHES

As for God, his way is perfect: The LORD's word is flawless; he shields all who take refuge in him. —Psalm 18:30 (NIV)

Our home's former owners had carelessly spread bark to cover over the flower beds, hoping for a quick sale.

"That's what people do," I complained.

However, sensing God's will, we bought the forty-five-year-old house, with all of its problems and potential.

The place made me ask: what was I smoothing over in my own life, trying to look good?

Beside the driveway, a patch of fist-sized rocks lay infested with tall weeds. Elsewhere, dozens of hosta plants created a lush jungle of disorganization. The front sidewalk's arbor leaned, warning passersby that it might fall. In the backyard, years of old charcoal briquette ashes had been dumped into a shallow hole.

I pondered what ashes remain tucked in the corners of my life.

My wife and I threw away the charred briquettes, smoothing new soil over the hole.

"Beauty for ashes," I whispered. "Better already."

Next, we tackled the rocks beside the driveway and planted new grass.

From across the street, our new neighbors called out, "Sure looks better since you guys moved in!"

Like improving a garden, the Eternal Gardener is ever at work in our lives. He's planting new seeds, clearing out rubbish, pulling weeds. We are better already since He moved in, and all His ways are good.

God, thank You for the continual, sanctifying work
You are doing in my life. Amen.
—Durwood Smith

GROWING IN FAITH

Today as you walk or drive through your neighborhood, look at the efforts your neighbors have made to beautify their properties. Thank God for them and for the beauty He plants in you.

A BRUISED REED

A bruised reed he will not break, and a smoldering wick he will not snuff out, till he has brought justice through to victory.
—Matthew 12:20 (NIV)

I almost drove past the wilted weeds. I assumed the homeowner set them out for trash day, but a scrap of cardboard taped to a stick caught my attention: "Free Tiger Lilies."

I knew nothing about tiger lilies, but I assumed, based on their name, they should not look like bedraggled twigs. I parked the car to examine them, but they appeared beyond saving.

Something about tiger lilies tweaked a memory. Tiger Lily was the Native American name given to my granddaughter, Haley, fifteen years ago, during a traditional naming ceremony.

Haley was a preemie. She spent the first several weeks of her life in the neonatal intensive care unit of the hospital. Her tiny limbs, much like these lilies, seemed too fragile to touch, as we waited and prayed that she would survive and thrive.

I opened the hatchback and scooped the fragile pile into my arms. At home, my husband and I planted them in a bare spot of land next to our deck.

Months later, my husband called me outside.

"Come look at the tiger lilies!" he said.

They had bloomed into flowers that now lived up to their name, just as Haley had. The petals were a vibrant reddish orange, red like my granddaughter's hair.

Like her, they had not only survived but also thrived.

Lord, thank You for Your amazing ability to revive us and help us thrive. Amen.
—Kristy Dewberry

GROWING IN FAITH

Have there been times when you felt like a "bruised reed"? Take a moment to remind yourself how God healed and revived you.

SOFTEN THE CLAY

"And I will give you a new heart, and a new spirit I will put within you. And I will remove the heart of stone from your flesh and give you a heart of flesh." —Ezekiel 36:26 (ESV)

Fall is the perfect time to plant perennial bulbs for spring blooms.

But the patch I chose to plant this year had a hidden surprise. As I dug my trowel into the earth, I quickly hit clay. Under the shallow layer of topsoil lay a thick, impenetrable mass. I pulled out the garden hose and thoroughly soaked the area, giving it time to absorb the water before repeating the process several times. Once the water had softened the clay, I was able to dig deeply, break up chunks with additional organic material, and finally create a suitable place for my bulbs to thrive.

I thought of how often my heart is hardened by the cares of this world. Packed down under the stress of daily life. Plagued by hurts buried deeply. *Impenetrable.*

Like my flower bed, I might look fine from the outside. I can put on a good show for those around me. But Jesus knows when my heart is hard and when nothing can be planted there. And when it is, I need to soak in the Word of God and let His Truth sink deeply into me. He softens my heart so that He can help me grow in beautiful ways.

Jesus, show me where my heart has become hardened.
Give me a new heart and a new spirit, Lord.
—Candee Fick

GROWING IN FAITH

Listen to worship music during your commute or around the house, and let the truth of God's love soak into your heart today.

CUCUMBER ART

Then God said, "Let the land produce vegetation: seed-bearing plants and trees on the land that bear fruit with seed in it, according to their various kinds." And it was so. The land produced vegetation: plants bearing seed according to their kinds and trees bearing fruit with seed in it according to their kinds. And God saw that it was good. —Genesis 1:11–12 (NIV)

"Mom, can I come home and get a cucumber and some tomatoes from your garden?" my daughter, Jo, asked over the phone.

"Sure! I have plenty!" I was excited to share, privately congratulating myself for raising her right. Now that she was an adult, she clearly *liked* all those vegetables I cajoled her into eating as a child.

"I only need one cucumber and a few cherry tomatoes," Jo said. "I want to paint them for an art exhibit next month."

Chuckling, I hung up.

Boy, was I wrong! I should have known better: Jo always hated cucumbers.

A month later, I stood staring at a painting of my cucumber. It was taller than me! *That's the biggest, most beautiful cucumber I have ever grown,* I thought. I marveled at my daughter's talent and the creativity it took to see a simple vegetable in such a way. While I just thought of it as food, Jo had seen its beauty. The multiple shades of green and yellow, the oval plumpness, the glory of God's creation.

And it reminded me that all of Creation is beautiful if we stop and look at it through God's eyes.

Jesus, thank You for the beauty of the natural world.

—Beth Gormong

GROWING IN FAITH

Take a short walk today and thank God for His creation. Look around with His loving eyes.

MAKING ROOM FOR BEAUTY

The heavens declare the glory of God; And the firmament shows His handiwork. —Psalm 19:1 (NKJV)

Clicking out of yet another specialty seed website, I sighed. I was on the hunt for a specific variety of sunflower after having seen it at my local public garden—and, it seemed, so was everyone else. It had taken me a month to track down the variety's name based on the picture I'd snapped, and I wasn't prepared for the disappointment of it being sold out everywhere I looked.

After a decade of dogmatically declaring that every plant must be useful, meaning food-producing, to warrant a coveted spot in my fenced-in, carefully tended, vegetable-only garden, I've changed my tune dramatically.

How boring my garden looked before I deemed zinnias, marigolds, morning glories, snapdragons, and so many other flowers worthy of a bit of space in the midst of peppers, tomatoes, and squash. The riot of color caused by my annual flowers is unruly, uncoordinated, and breathtakingly beautiful. The untidy bouquets from my garden flowers bring deep joy to my soul in ways vegetables do not.

In a world that values productivity and accomplishment above all else, I fell headlong into that same trap in my garden. Undervaluing beauty simply for beauty's sake, I forgot that God creates *both* the useful and the lovely. Gardens without flowers is like a life lived focused purely on accomplishment. It's functional but missing the full magnificence of what God intended for us.

Heavenly Father, remind me to appreciate beauty in Your creation, remembering that You are behind sunrises, flower petals, and everything beautiful in between.

—Julie Fisk

GROWING IN FAITH

Look for beauty today, thanking God for His creative masterpieces.

WHAT DOES YOUR GARDEN TELL OTHERS?

So whether you eat or drink or whatever you do, do it all for the glory of God. —1 Corinthians 10:31 (NIV)

A vegetable garden isn't merely a section of ground used for growing food. That would be like saying a painting is just a canvas with colors on it. More accurately, a garden is an expression of a gardener, like a painting is an expression of the artist.

A gardening mentor of mine once said, "You can tell the state of a person's heart by the way their field looks."

When people look at my garden, they are learning something about me. I am preaching a message about the God I say I serve.

That doesn't always mean my garden looks perfect. Sometimes it is reflecting the fact that we just had twin babies and have spent several weeks at the hospital. At other times, it reflects my lack of faithfulness and my overambition. But if I approach my garden with the heart attributes of Jesus—His humility, faithfulness, and unselfishness—they will start to show through my methods, management, and ministry to others. This gives me an opportunity to point to Jesus when answering people's questions about my garden.

Our garden can be one of the most impactful sermons we preach to our neighbors.

Jesus, even as gardeners, we are Your ambassadors of hope to a world that needs You. Show us how You want Your heart to transform our gardens into vibrant expressions of Your abundance, healing, beauty, and forgiveness. Amen.

—Noah Sanders

GROWING IN FAITH

Look at the garden of your life and write down what messages it might be conveying to strangers. Ask God to show you how to better reflect His humility, faithfulness, and unselfishness.

BOUNTIFUL HARVEST

Whoever sows to please their flesh, from the flesh will reap destruction; whoever sows to please the Spirit, from the Spirit will reap eternal life.
—Galatians 6:8 (NIV)

One of the ways in which my gardening skills grew last year was in learning to save seeds for the following year. As the new gardening season began, I took great satisfaction and delight in sowing those saved seeds.

When my radishes, grown from my own radish seeds, were ready to harvest, I was surprised to see that some of them weren't the red, globe-shaped vegetable I expected. Instead, they were white and cylindrical. Although they were not the radishes I expected, they were still radishes—and they became my new favorite kind because of their taste and texture.

The same is true in the spiritual realm. God's Word is clear: I reap what I sow, even when the result isn't what I expected.

My most important and difficult decisions often come down to one of two choices. Either I do what *I* really want to do or I do what I know to be the right course according to God's standards. A decision for pleasing myself might reap some temporary satisfaction, but it can also bring unwanted consequences. Like all temporal things, it can't last; it can even draw me further from the Lord.

In contrast, sowing seeds of love and obedience, things that line up with God's Word, brings joy. Like my delicious white radishes, they also bring unexpected surprise!

Empower me, Lord, by Your Spirit, to sow seed in accordance with Your ways. Amen.
—Cathy Bryant

GROWING IN FAITH

With each opportunity to "sow" today, be mindful of what kind of "seed" you are planting.

THE POWER OF COMMUNITY

Each of you should use whatever gift you have received to serve others, as faithful stewards of God's grace in its various forms. —1 Peter 4:10 (NIV)

My daughter, Aurora, gently cups her fingers over the dried-out red prairie coneflower blossom. Then, just as I showed her—as my mother showed me—she pulls the flower from bottom to top, and each tiny seed relents, falling gracefully into a pile in her hand.

That week, I take some of the seeds to our local Native Plant Seed Swap. I browse tables with seeds contributed by gardeners across our community: showy milkweed for monarch migration, chokeberries for robins and black-capped chickadees, Indian blanket flower with its fiery red petals dipped in yellow. Dozens of people browse the aisles of tables, excitedly picking up envelopes of seeds to bring home.

Growing up in the church, I've witnessed the power of group effort. Many times my family and I have been the recipients of the hospitality and love offered by a group of people with shared beliefs and convictions. I see it here, too, amid this group of gardeners. Our reasons may differ, but many of us share a deep passion for preserving the beauty of Creation. Alone, my little pollinator garden might not offer much. But, strung together, our efforts have an exponential impact. Trading seeds with one another from one season for the next, we join in the practice of land stewardship and the act of preserving all that is lovely.

God, thank You for the community You've placed me in. Show me how to bless others with the gifts You've given me. Amen.

—Eryn Lynum

GROWING IN FAITH

This week, reach out in love to someone in your community.

The garden reconciles human art and wild nature, hard work and deep pleasure, spiritual practice and the material world. It is a magical place because it is not divided.

THOMAS MOORE, WRITER

DESPERATE TIMES, DESPERATE MEASURES

You will keep him in perfect peace, Whose mind is stayed on You.
—Isaiah 26:3 (NKJV)

After dinner, I tried to relax on the sofa with my husband, but I was too squirmy.

"I need to confess something," I said.

I'd been worked up for a week over a frustrating situation. I'd kept it to myself, thinking by now I should know how to manage anxiety. I'd spent time with Jesus each morning. I'd prayed. Why wasn't my faith enough to keep me from worry?

"Could you need even more time in His presence?" my hubby asked.

His question reminded me of The Great Tomato Fiasco. When we moved from California's mild coastal zone to Oregon's arid high desert, I knew gardening would be more challenging. So I figured I'd begin with something foolproof. I potted a tomato start and staked it. It half-heartedly grew. Fruit appeared, green and small and rock-hard, but then it refused to gain much size or ripen.

I'd assumed that what worked in the past, in a different climate, would work again. Expecting success, I gave up at the first sign of trouble without even asking for advice. Later I learned that a plant confined to a container under the high desert's dry summer heat is under extra stress—requiring extra attention and extra water.

In extra-stressful conditions I, too, need more attention from and time with my Gardener. Hubby was right. My anxiety level called for more Living Water.

What worked in the past wouldn't see me through today's trying circumstances.

Father, when anxiety reigns, I commit to guzzle rather than sip from Your fountain of Living Water.
—Kit Tosello

GROWING IN FAITH

Memorize Isaiah 26:3. Write it on a wooden stake for your garden or for a houseplant.

LOVE YOUR ENEMIES

But I tell you, love your enemies and pray for those who persecute you.
—Matthew 5:44 (NIV)

For gardeners, weeds are our nemeses. They are invasive and creep into our gardens by lying dormant in the ground for years or sneaking in with the mulch or manure. They compete for the resources of the intended plants. In the juvenile stage, they mimic the desired plants. You must distinguish between them to control them.

People bring me weeds to identify. I need to know about them so I can provide the proper methods to eradicate them. To become familiar with weeds, I developed what I call "weed therapy." I make sure I know the weeds in my own garden. Ones I don't recognize require using plant identification resources. I learn to appreciate weeds as I study them, and every year, I can more easily identify them.

The question is, how well do you know *your* weeds?

Jesus told His disciples to "love your enemies." To love someone, you have to get to know them. You have to discern why they oppose you. As you learn more about people who are your "enemies," you might find that you share common ground with them. As you show love toward them, you can break down some of the barriers between you and perhaps even see them as flowers, not weeds.

Weeds are just plants out of place. Sometimes animosity between people comes down to being misunderstood or growing in an unexpected place.

Lord God, give us the ability to love and pray for our enemies and reach them with the same love You had for us when we were Your enemy. Let them identify us by our love. Amen.
—Ben Cooper

GROWING IN FAITH

Shower those opposed to you with love and see what blossoms.

PREPARING FOR THE HARVEST

This is to my Father's glory, that you bear much fruit, showing yourselves to be my disciples. —John 15:8 (NIV)

I didn't grow up eating bell peppers, but I really enjoy growing them. One day, a few years back, I was in my garden when a pepper plant caught my eye. It was producing the beginning of an ambitious pepper. That wasn't unusual. But what drew my attention was the size of the plant. It was still quite small, and the fruit was pulling the whole plant over to the ground. I went over and plucked off the fruit, admonishing the plant in my mind, "If you want to produce a lot of peppers, you need to put that energy into growing a bit bigger first."

Many gardeners know that the production of fruiting plants like peppers, tomatoes, and even blueberries and apples will be better in the long run if you keep them from producing fruit until they reach a certain size. I am a bit like that pepper plant sometimes. So often I want God to do great things in my life, but admittedly I need to grow first. I need to learn to be faithful with little before God entrusts me with more.

God is the perfect gardener, and the lesson of that pepper plant helps remind me to be patient as God helps me grow in preparation for the fruit He wants to produce.

Lord, I want fruit in my life. Please help me to grow in my own walk with You so I can be ready to handle the opportunities and responsibilities You bring in the future. Amen.

—Noah Sanders

GROWING IN FAITH

Today identify an area of your life that you want God to bring to fruition and take it to Him.

CELEBRATING WITH SUNFLOWERS

"For six years sow your fields, and for six years prune your vineyards and gather their crops. But in the seventh year the land is to have a year of sabbath rest, a sabbath to the Lord. *Do not sow your fields or prune your vineyards."* —Leviticus 25:3–4 (NIV)

Driving through the Kansas countryside, most of the year you'll see cornstalks, soy, and wheat. I grew up in the Midwest, and there's something soothing about seeing those waving stalks for me. But even more beautiful are the flowers Kansas is known for—sunflowers.

When I was growing up, I worked on a friend's farm in western Kansas. I learned that once crops are harvested, some farmers plant sunflowers.

The glorious benefit is vast fields of gorgeous flowers, but the more practical benefit is they allow the soil to rest. Sunflowers produce seeds and keep pollinators nearby.

Farmers can choose simply to leave fields empty during the non-growing season, but many plant sunflowers instead. Some do it for their beauty, some to celebrate successful harvests.

As I think of the sunflower-filled Kansas fields, I also think about how I choose to fill my own life when it feels like nothing is growing, when it feels like *I* am not growing. *Am I choosing to fill difficult or dormant days with sunflowers or letting my life go fallow?*

I may not, for the moment, be planting success, but I can still celebrate with a field of bright sunflowers.

Lord, please help me find joy and beauty in my life even when it feels as if nothing new is happening and nothing is growing. Amen.

—Amy Barnes

GROWING IN FAITH

Take a look at how you can find brightness in the off seasons of life.

RESCUED PLANTS AND PEOPLE

For he has rescued us from the dominion of darkness and brought us into the kingdom of the Son he loves. —Colossians 1:13 (NIV)

Oh, you poor thing, I thought as I spotted the bedraggled, broken coleus on the garden store's clearance rack. Coleus is one of my favorite plants, with its bright varicolored leaves and stalks of tiny pastel blooms. I *had* to rescue this unloved one. The thought of it dying in a dumpster was unbearable.

I tucked my languishing plant between bags of groceries on the passenger seat and drove home carefully. I snapped off the dead stalks. With love mixed with pity, I planted it in a huge pot next to the garage.

"Here you go, buddy," I said. "The perfect combination of shade and sun."

Each time the coleus put out a new leaf or stood a bit taller, I chirped, "I'm proud of you." By summer's end, my once-forgotten friend had grown to a lush beauty, overflowing its pot.

One crisp fall afternoon, my husband, Kevin, lugged the huge coleus into the house for the winter. I knew Kev was as thrilled with the plant's transformation as I was. We placed it on the floor of the dining room, where filtered sun would keep it warm and alive until spring. I sighed in gratification as I gazed at my now-vigorous rescue plant.

This must be the joy God feels when He gazes at each of His rescue children.

Dear Lord, only a love like Yours could see the potential in our sagging, lost souls. Thank You for giving us new life.

—Jeanette Levellie

GROWING IN FAITH

Next time you're shopping, find a castaway plant and rescue it, reflecting on how God has brought *you* back to life.

EXPERIENCING A LABYRINTH

"But small is the gate and narrow the road that leads to life, and only a few find it." —Matthew 7:14 (NIV)

Yesterday, my husband and I visited a sculpture garden that included a labyrinth. Unlike a hedge maze, this was a ground-level path marked out by pavers, so we could see that we were aiming toward a beautiful tree that rose in the center. Surrounded by shade trees, the clearing smelled of spring rain, while birds sang.

As we followed the path, it seemed to head toward the tree but then doubled back. Another turn led in a wide circle around the border of the area. As long as we continued to follow the path, even though it seemed to switch in random directions, we could eventually reach the tree without stepping off the trail. There were no dead ends.

As we slowly walked, accepting the switchbacks and pattern, I prayed. I realized how frustrated I often am when the quickest and easiest path isn't Christ's plan for me.

Sometimes in my walk of faith, I have a clear focus on the final aim. Jesus is leading me on a path that will take me to eternal life. That tree of life is visible even as my path winds. But when my steps seem to backtrack, I can become frustrated.

The labyrinth walk reminded me to trust His plan for my life and to look up frequently to see the reminders of where He is guiding me.

Lord, I confess that sometimes I feel like I'm wandering in circles. But I trust You to guide me. Amen.

—Sharon Hinck

GROWING IN FAITH

Take a walk today and use it as a time of prayer. Thank Jesus for the way He guides our steps and directs our paths.

SAVING THE WORLD, ONE PLANT AT A TIME

Rescue the weak and the needy; deliver them from the hand of the wicked.
—Psalm 82:4 (NIV)

My husband, Don, can spend hours at the do-it-yourself warehouse store while I trudge behind him like a petulant toddler, whining, "How much longer?" I was on the verge of throwing myself onto the floor in a full-blown tantrum recently when I noticed the gardening section.

It was off season and most of the plants were marked 75 percent off. I can't pass up a good deal, so I told Don I'd browse while he finished shopping. He looked positively gleeful to be rid of me as he raced toward the home repair section. The plants were bedraggled-looking and pitiful. I wandered up and down the aisles, and then I asked an employee what they do with the ones that don't sell.

"We throw them out," he said, with what I imagined to be an evil grin.

My heart broke a little. I imagined each plant, like an unwanted dog in an animal shelter, hoping an owner will arrive and issue a stay of execution and bring him home.

When Don returned to the gardening section, he seemed surprised to see me with a shopping cart full of wilted plants, but he didn't say a thing as we headed to the checkout.

"I just couldn't leave them there," I confessed.

Our next stop was the pet store. A big banner announced it was Adopt-a-Dog Day.

"You're waiting in the car," Don said, laughing.

Father, guide us when we see those in need of help that we not turn away but that we show compassion.
—Kristy Dewberry

GROWING IN FAITH

Today pray for someone who is hurting, and let them know you are bringing their concerns to God.

COMPARE OR SHARE

Don't compare yourself with others. Each of you must take responsibility for doing the creative best you can with your own life.
—Galatians 6:5 (MSG)

"On my walk today, I saw the most beautiful garden," I told my husband, Kevin. "It was like an artist's palette, with flowers in a dozen different colors."

I sighed, wishing my garden were that stunning. But with two jobs, I don't have time to create a landscape fit for a magazine cover, so I enjoy other people's labors. And I relish my own simple plot of earth.

It wasn't always like this. In the past, I made myself miserable as I gazed on a neighbor's thriving vegetable patch or flower oasis. Because I compared my own modest garden with someone's creative landscaping, I couldn't find joy in either garden, both lovely in their own ways.

So Jesus took pity on me. He showed me that if I appreciated the land He gave me and did my best to improve it, I'd be free to enjoy what He'd given others. It worked! The more I delighted in my little garden, the better I've been free to applaud others' work.

This fun principle applies not only to veggies, flowers, and trees but also to anything I'm tempted to envy in someone else's life. The trap of comparison leads to discontentment. Choosing contentment and rejoicing in others' achievements leads to fullness of joy.

And Jesus is all about joy.

Lord, I appreciate all the gifts of creativity You share with Your children. Please help me develop joy in what You've given others and contentment in all that I have. Amen.
—Jeanette Levellie

GROWING IN FAITH

Next time you see a gorgeous garden, thank God, and thank the gardener who grew it.

SMASHING PUMPKINS

Flee the evil desires of youth and pursue righteousness, faith, love, and peace, along with those who call on the Lord out of a pure heart.
—2 Timothy 2:22 (NIV)

Just before Halloween, my tiny patch of pumpkins was ripening. I'd never grown gourds before, and I was proud. About the size of bowling balls, all four nestled on an unfenced side of my house. My two little grandchildren planned to carve and decorate them for the big night.

But the day we planned to harvest, I stood at the patch in shock. Overnight, someone had smashed every single one.

My youngest grandson wailed, "How will we have a happy Halloween?"

I had to think fast.

"Don't worry," I said. "God has lots of pumpkins!"

I bundled them into the car, and we headed to a local farm that offered hayrides to a pumpkin patch. When the children saw the sea of orange out in the fields, they squealed in delight. Each chose two pumpkins to take home, and soon they were happily carving and decorating them. I couldn't help but notice how God turned evil into good. He often redeems our losses with far better outcomes.

The people who destroyed my pumpkin patch couldn't stop God from supplying more pumpkins than I could ever grow and more happiness than I had imagined. My young grandsons had a ball on Halloween, proudly displaying their beautiful pumpkins. The youngest one's grin was as wide as a jack-o'-lantern's when he said, "God grows the bestest punkins ever."

I had to say amen to that!

Lord, when bad things happen, help me look for the good You can bring.
—Linda S. Clare

GROWING IN FAITH

Today ask God to show you how you can share bounty with someone facing misfortune or loss.

BURST INTO BLOOM

Like the crocus, it will burst into bloom; it will rejoice greatly and shout for joy. —Isaiah 35:1–2 (NIV)

Have you ever watched time-lapse videos of flowers blooming? They are fast-forward videos of flowers coming into blossom. We can see the petals opening and the flowers turning their heads toward the sun. It is such a wondrous sight.

In the garden, we don't get to see the precise moment flowers blossom. We plant the flowers, watch buds come up, and then one day, seemingly all of a sudden, the blossoms are there. It brings us such joy to see the faces of our flowers in the garden. But to see the blooms quickly in a video is like watching fireworks! I can't help but smile.

Nothing lifts my heart like flowers in bloom. That's why I love the passage above from Isaiah. Isaiah has given the flower human attributes. A crocus cannot really rejoice or shout, but *I* can. When I see the crocus bloom, then I certainly feel joy in my heart; it reminds me of the joy I have in the Lord.

Crocuses bloom in the spring, the season of Easter, and they are a wonderful reminder of all God's glory. Sometimes I even have snow on the ground when my crocuses reach their blossoms toward the sky.

"Spring is coming," they seem to shout. "God is here, and life is good." It certainly makes my heart burst into bloom with joy and thanksgiving.

God, I rejoice in Your creation! Thank You for the gift of Your Son.

—Heather Jepsen

GROWING IN FAITH

What joy is bursting in your heart today?
Say a prayer thanking God for new life.

Good gardening means being alive to the web of life.

JOHN B.E. SIMMONS, GARDEN CURATOR

THE BLESSINGS OF GENEROUS GARDENING

"With the measure you use, it will be measured to you."
—Mark 4:24 (NIV)

I value my compost. After several months of careful management, the resulting pile of rich, brown organic matter produces satisfaction when I look at it. Naturally, I am very judicious in my application of compost in the garden. When I go to apply it, I always feel a bit stingy. One of my desires is to reflect God's nature in the way I approach my garden, and stingy definitely isn't one of His character traits. So, this last year, I decided to try to be more generous and see what happened.

Normally I would put one wheelbarrow load of compost on a twenty-foot-long garden bed before planting a crop of arugula. Instead, I put two loads on only half a bed and planted it. Incredibly, due to high-quality harvests and regrowth, this generous application resulted in three to four times the yield from that ten-foot-long section of arugula as I had been getting from twenty feet before!

Over the years, I have found this principle of taking my limited resources and focusing them more generously on a smaller garden and limited number of plants has always resulted in better yields and increased beauty.

God loves us to reflect His generosity and will always measure back to us more than we give.

Lord, You are extravagantly generous. Please protect me from a stingy or greedy attitude. Give me faith to be extravagant in my giving, knowing that I can never outgive You.
—Noah Sanders

GROWING IN FAITH

Is there an area of your life where you might be missing the blessing of being generous? Ask God to show you how to focus your time, talents, and resources to display His extravagant generosity.

PLANTED IN HIS WORD

"The grass withers and the flowers fall, but the word of our God endures forever." —Isaiah 40:8 (NIV)

My first home was a sweet little rowhouse just outside of colonial Ellicott City, Maryland, a stone's throw from the Patapsco River, which flows into the Chesapeake Bay. I had a postage-stamp-sized garden in the backyard with rich riverbed soil. To my amazement, my novice green thumb raised a bounty of beautiful tomatoes, zucchini, peppers, and lush basil plants that kept me in fresh pesto for months. The crops grew nearly effortlessly.

My next home was on nearly four acres in West Virginia, just outside the quaint historic town of Berkeley Springs. Emboldened by my earlier success, I was excited to greatly increase my garden size. There, however, apart from being overly ambitious in the scale, I faced a number of challenges. These included rocky and malnourished soil, tenacious weeds, and all kinds of critters like deer and bunnies. In the end, I gave up and settled for a small raised-bed garden. The "soil" at my West Virginia home just didn't allow for my dream vegetable garden.

I liken this to my life in Christ. When I plant myself in the rich soil of God's Word—studying, absorbing, believing, and obeying—He can produce a beautiful, hardy crop of spiritual fruit in me.

Dear Jesus, please enrich the soil of my understanding of You and Your Word. Open my ears to what You're trying to teach me and help me produce a bountiful crop for Your glory. Amen.

—Isabella Campolattaro

GROWING IN FAITH

Write down two or three ways you can better or more consistently immerse yourself in His Word, "nourishing your soil with Him," then make a plan to do so.

CUT THROUGH THE SUCKERS

But Martha was distracted by all the preparations that had to be made. . . . "Martha, Martha," the Lord answered, "you are worried and upset about many things, but few things are needed—or indeed only one. Mary has chosen what is better, and it will not be taken away from her."
—Luke 10:40–42 (NIV)

While cleaning out one of my flower beds, I discovered that my cherry tree had put up several offshoots, and the largest was already an inch in diameter. Left unchecked, those new trees would continue to steal nutrients, water, and eventually light from the original tree, thereby weakening it and making it susceptible to disease. The immediate and necessary solution was to grab the pruners.

As I cut away the competition so the primary tree could be the focus again, I was reminded of how cluttered my life had become. A multitude of distractions was stealing my time, energy, and focus away from my family, mission, and core values, and like Martha's tasks, they were adding to my overall stress level.

However, Jesus's answer to Martha's complaints was a gentle reminder to focus on the few things that are truly needed, like a solid relationship with God, followed by bonds with family or friends and diligence in a profession.

Like pruning around my tree, when I'm able to focus my energy on what's truly important, I am less worried about or upset by the rest.

Jesus, reveal the distractions that are keeping me from focusing on the things that matter most and give me the strength to set them aside.
—Candee Fick

GROWING IN FAITH

Today replace one distracting or time-wasting activity (such as scrolling through social media or watching television) with a purposeful one (like having a real conversation or spending time reading Scripture).

GOD'S RESTORING POWER

Be alert and of sober mind. Your enemy the devil prowls around like a roaring lion looking for someone to devour. —1 Peter 5:8 (NIV)

On an early spring morning, my husband, Jason, and I were surprised to find a "Yard of the Month" sign staked beside our driveway courtesy of our homeowners association. After years of work, our front yard had finally become a beautiful portrait of God's creation. Flower beds, outlined with the perfect shade of landscape bricks, hugged the perimeter of our home. Dozens of shrubs had matured into seamless hedges that reached right up to the window line. And our "statement trees"—several live oaks and two queen palms—had withstood enough winters and storms to prove that they had been worth the investment. We took photos of the sign in our freshly mowed grass and celebrated the unexpected compliment.

The next morning, however, we awoke to a very different scene. Our flower beds were in complete disarray. Plants had been uprooted, and dirt and mulch littered the lawn. Flowers lay limp like fallen soldiers. Sometime in the night, an army of armadillos had attacked.

The destruction felt personal, as if the armadillos had read "Yard of the Month" and targeted our home, and it reminded me of the many times I'd been sucker punched by attacks from the devil. However, as we cleaned the debris, replanted the flowers, and hid armadillo traps strategically in the bushes, I found peace in remembering that God can restore anything the devil destroys.

The Lord's beauty will always prevail.

Lord, when the enemy attacks, help me to remember Your restoring power. Amen.

—Emily E. Ryan

GROWING IN FAITH

Identify any areas of your life where you are vulnerable to attacks from the enemy and pray for the Lord's protection.

LORD OF ALL

But the godly shall flourish like palm trees... For they are transplanted into the Lord's own garden and are under his personal care.
—Psalm 92:12–13 (TLB)

I imagine my neighbor secretly whispering about me, watching me month after month, walking around my garden.

"Here we go again," he might be saying. "The old guy is out in his yard, talking to himself, yet again."

If he is, that's okay. The truth is, I'm communing in spirit with God's stunning creation and with God Himself.

When I peer into a giant orange poppy bloom, with its cupped tissue paper–like petals and sooty black center, I mumble, "No human made this happen."

When I detect a buzzing bumblebee deep inside a zucchini blossom, I don't pretend to understand how God crafted its instincts.

I marvel that a butternut squash is so strange and different though still a squash.

I know my garden: seeds, soil, vines, shrubs, annuals, and perennials. I know where they came from, when they were planted, when they'll bloom, and even when they will die. I even know how to take care of what's left of them after they're dead.

Our loving Heavenly Father tends to His garden of souls too. He knows where we came from, when we were planted into His garden, when we will bloom, and even when we'll die.

As I talk with the plants in my own garden, my words and heart are full of worship, all year long.

Oh, Creator God, all Your ways are perfect. I trust You with everything.
—Durwood Smith

GROWING IN FAITH

Spend time talking with God today. Thank Him for knowing your past, present, and future.

PRODUCE BY RESTING

"Observe the Sabbath day by keeping it holy, as the LORD your God has commanded you. Six days you shall labor and do all your work, but the seventh day is a sabbath to the LORD your God."
—Deuteronomy 5:12–14a (NIV)

There's nothing quite as disappointing as tending the garden and finding bugs in broccoli, yellowing leaves on pepper plants, and black spots on tomatoes. Of all the potential solutions, many claim that crop rotation, or moving different plant families into different locations each year, can reduce damage from pests, limit the development of diseases, and replenish soil nutrients. The practice increases garden productivity, especially if alternated with fallow periods where the land is deliberately left to rest and regenerate instead of being cultivated.

Like the weekly Sabbath day, God knew that periods of regular rest for the land was equally beneficial. During the Sabbath year, the fields and vineyards grew "volunteer" crops that fed the poor, while any excess that fell to the ground became natural compost material that restored nutrients, moisture, and microorganisms to the soil. In addition, the people had to trust that God would provide for their personal needs since the sixth year's harvest had to last until the eighth year's crops were ready.

It's counterintuitive to think that I can produce *more* by doing *less*.

And by seeing the results in my garden, I am reminded that I need to do the same in my life.

Jesus, teach me how to rest and trust You to multiply my productivity in the other hours of the week.
—Candee Fick

GROWING IN FAITH

Clear your schedule and plan ahead so that the next Sabbath is truly a day of rest for you.

WHAT ARE YOU PLANTING?

He will also send you rain for the seed you sow in the ground.
—Isaiah 30:23 (NIV)

Recently, while reading the verse above, I visualized how the rain God sends waters a seed, causing it to break open in the dark, grow roots into the ground, and shoot upward through the soil. Then a question arose in my mind that stopped me in my tracks: *What seeds am I sowing that will grow in the soil of my life?*

If every thought I have or action I take grows deep roots and gains strength, do I want them breaking through the topsoil and unfurling into the world? Certainly not on the days when I'm impatient and frustrated. There's enough discord in the world without me planting more. Looking at my life this way, I'm more mindful now of how I behave, wanting to add only kindness and grace to the garden of God's world.

The only way to achieve that is to sort through the seeds of my heart in the presence of Jesus. He'll help me see what attitudes and behavior will lead to weeds, choking out any good I want to contribute. If I offer them to Him, He'll toss them away before I have the chance to plant them. He'll also help me identify the gifts and beauty He's graced me with, encouraging me to plant from that abundance, making my life a unique and pleasing bouquet for Him.

Sower of Gifts, help me to eliminate what I don't want to take root so I plant only what is pleasing to You. Amen.
—Claire McGarry

GROWING IN FAITH

Think about the words you've said and the things you've done today. Do you want them to "take root"?

WAITING FOR BULBS

If I go up to the heavens, you are there; if I make my bed in the depths, you are there. —Psalm 139:8 (NIV)

That October, I planned for spring. Our soil is rocky and full of clay, so the digging wasn't easy. I bent a hand spade trying to dig holes for my bulbs. But I knew that daffodils and tulips must slumber deep in the cold ground to put on God's spring parade.

My muscles burned as I excavated. The spade clunked against stones lining the soil. It was worth it to dig extra-deep places for my garden's star attractions. Finally, the bulb bed was ready.

I dropped in the teardrop-shaped bulbs—heads up—and covered them over, then tucked in some cool-weather pansies on top. The cheery yellows and purples would remind me where to look for the grand opening in March or April.

Soon, an early snow dusted the pansies. The winter months can sometimes feel eternal, but a glance at the brave pansies reminded me of their hidden promise. Each time I gazed out at the bulb bed, I thought of all the ways God nudges me to let go of the past and anticipate spring's new birth.

I'm glad I don't have to live underground, but seasonal darkness gives me time to press in close to God for extra warmth and light.

Next spring, I hope my efforts will burst forth and dazzle me after the long hibernation. For now, I'm content to sip warm cocoa and snuggle up to our Father while I wait for the coming season.

Lord, help me let go of the past and look to the future.

—Linda S. Clare

GROWING IN FAITH

Today consider planting some bulbs to remind yourself that spring will come.

SWEET GRAPES

"I am the true grapevine, and my Father is the gardener. He cuts off every branch of mine that doesn't produce fruit, and he prunes the branches that do bear fruit so they will produce even more." —John 15:1–2 (NLT)

I tried planting a grapevine once. It stretched meager vines up the side of the house and produced only a few sour grapes. With my unskilled care, the whole plant died before the next spring.

Likewise, sometimes my efforts in other areas of life seem to produce nothing but a few sour grapes. I'm tempted by envy for those who are healthier and able to volunteer more than me. I grow discouraged with lack of progress in my writing projects. I long to be a warm and loving presence to my family and friends but often chase my own selfish needs instead.

I'm grateful that God calls Himself a gardener and that He is far more skilled than I am. He prunes away activities that wear me out. He gently shapes the direction of my work so it can bear the most fruit. He doesn't give up, even when my heart is sour. He forgives and grants nourishment to sweeten the fruit I long to bear for Him.

I need His pruning work in my spiritual life so that I can grow to be more like Him.

Dear Heavenly Father, please prune away the vines in my life that don't produce. Please help my soul to draw sweetness from clinging to Your Son. Amen.

—Sharon Hinck

GROWING IN FAITH

Taste something sour, like a lemon. Ask God to show you any sour attitudes in need of transformation. Then taste something sweet, like a spoonful of honey, and ask Him to produce sweet fruit in your life.

A GIFT OF ROSE HIPS

And do not forget to do good and to share with others, for with such sacrifices God is pleased. —Hebrews 13:16 (NIV)

I reached for a lone red rose hip, trying to avoid the thorns without much success. An Abert's squirrel, with his tasseled ears and bushy gray tail, scolded me from the branches of a ponderosa pine as I searched the bush for one more elusive ripened sphere, about the size of a small pea.

"Do you have enough rose hips to make jelly this year?" my friend Laura asked, coming out from her cabin.

"No, I need more." I held up the small bagful I had picked that morning. "I'll add these to the ones I have in the freezer."

"Tough year for wild roses," Laura said. "Not enough rain."

I agreed, disappointed. I had hoped to make jelly at the end of the summer, after the flowers lost their pink petals and the seedpods had ripened. The slight hibiscus flavor and high concentration of vitamin C made it a nutritious fruit to forage near our cabin in northern Arizona.

Several weeks later, Laura surprised me with a large bag of rose hips she had gathered with her three grandchildren.

"They had a competition to see who could find the most," she said, brushing aside my thanks. "They'd like to taste the jelly after you make a batch."

"I'll give them a jar," I assured her.

The rosy-red offering cost no money, but I was touched by the currency of time and kindness my friend had spent on my behalf.

Jesus, may generosity ripen in my heart today.

—Lynne Hartke

GROWING IN FAITH

Today spend the currency of kindness on someone in need.

At the heart of gardening there is a belief in the miraculous.

MIRABEL OSLER, ENGLISH WRITER AND GARDEN DESIGNER

BETTER, NOT EASIER

Always give yourselves fully to the work of the Lord, because you know that your labor in the Lord is not in vain. —1 Corinthians 15:58 (NIV)

Had anyone told me how much work is involved in gardening, I never would have begun. Fortunately, I was blissfully naive when ordering my seeds. More so when buying a decrepit rototiller with no muffler from a suspiciously gleeful *ex*-gardener.

My wake-up call should have come when I started busting sod with "Old Shaky." By the end of the day, my back was spasming, my shoulders felt like rubber, and I was coughing up dirt.

Well, I thought, *at least the worst is over*. Not so much.

Twenty-four hours and a few ibuprofen later, I was back out there, stooping, bending, and kneeling to plant the seed. *Oh, my aching back!*

Surely now the worst is over, I thought.

But then came the cultivating, watering, and weeding.

And the rabbits, those "adorable" little rabbits. Tenderfoot that I was, tending that garden was the most intense labor of my life. The worst was *never* over. Every bit of it was atrociously hard work.

Yet sure enough, later that summer I found myself knee-deep in fresh sweet corn, juicy red tomatoes, and big yellow squash. That hard work produced a result!

Whether tasty vegetables, secure adult children, healthy relationships, or mature faith, no good thing is produced without effort.

The harvest does not come easily. But it does come.

Dear Jesus, I'm surprised by how much work it is to love God and others. Give me the strength to keep going so I can keep growing. Amen.

—Lawrence W. Wilson

GROWING IN FAITH

Attempt a difficult task or chore today, and thank God for the good that results from it.

A COLD-WEATHER OFFERING

"As the rain and the snow come down from heaven, and do not return to it without watering the earth and making it bud and flourish . . ."
—Isaiah 55:10 (NIV)

I wake to a cold November morning. Glancing out the window, our garden on the west side of the yard is shriveled. Composed of non-native annuals the kids chose for color, these flowers won't come back next year. Their time has come and gone.

Stepping outside to glimpse our native pollinator garden at the back side of the house, I'm surprised to find our firecracker penstemon still standing tall, boasting bright red blossoms. Yesterday was our first snow of the season. Most gardens seem to know, at this point, that the season is over—but not our native plants. Although a chill in the air has sapped our blossoms of most of their color, their stems remain vibrant green. Our blue grama and switchgrass look ready, even eager, for colder days. These plants are not surprised by Colorado's winters. They've thrived here on these prairies for far longer than I can imagine.

Our garden showcases to me a new type of resilience—a preparation and even *anticipation* for winter. As days grow shorter and a chilly darkness settles over the landscape, I heed wisdom from the flowers in our garden.

When we're where God has placed us, He helps us thrive no matter the season. Harsh conditions lend resilience to our roots. Abiding in His love and truth, the winter months of our lives are not an ending but a beginning.

God, I accept Your invitation of rest and empowerment this winter, knowing You are preparing me for beautiful things ahead.
—Eryn Lynum

GROWING IN FAITH

Today ask God to grow your faith through the winter months.

FIXING THE SOIL

"The Lord will guide you always; he will satisfy your needs in a sun-scorched land and will strengthen your frame. You will be like a well-watered garden, like a spring whose waters never fail."
—Isaiah 58:11 (NIV)

"Are you *sure* you want to plant a garden?" my husband asked. His question irritated me.

"Of course I do! You know my parents always had one," I said. "They saved so much grocery money by canning and freezing vegetables every year. It's always been my dream to do the same."

"We have clay here, not rich black soil like at your parents' place," he said. "It'll take a lot of work to get the soil healthy."

His words were discouraging, but I was stubborn. I forged ahead.

I had no idea that there were different types of soil and that my clay dirt would affect the way I garden, but I soon learned. When it rains, the ground stays wet for a long time. And when it's dry, it's hard as a brick. It's taken three years of composting, adding nutrients, tilling to break up the soil, and pulling deep-rooted weeds to get the garden soil in decent shape.

My clay soil reminds me of a particularly difficult time in my life when my soul felt dry and my heart hardened.

I'm glad God was stubborn with me and kept working on me, believing in the life in me. He didn't give up but kept pouring His love, forgiveness, and healing into me.

Jesus, You are the Master Gardener. You tend our souls and provide what we need to heal, grow, and become healthy.
—Beth Gormong

GROWING IN FAITH

Where might your heart, mind, or soul be dry and hard? Ask God to fill you with His healing water.

ALL FOR THE GOOD

"He who sits on the throne will shelter them with his presence."
—Revelation 7:15 (NIV)

Despite the crisp fall air today, I sat outside, wrapped in a blanket, trying to pray. As the wind blew through the trees, my eyes were caught by the twirling leaves showering down like pixie dust. It was mesmerizing. My appreciation of it became my prayer. I praised Jesus for the elaborate detail He's woven through nature.

Then it occurred to me that all those falling leaves were covering the garden I'd just cleared out and put to bed. As frustration began to take hold, I had to remind myself that God is always working for my good. I could see the falling leaves as a complication, or I could see them as God's perfect plan to shelter and protect my garden from the upcoming winter. I chose the latter and welcomed the array of colorful leaves that enveloped my garden like an intricate quilt.

It seems there's always another way to look at what life sends me. When things don't go my way, I need to stop and look at them from a different angle. Jesus is always sending His love to protect and prosper me, even amidst the difficulties. Every time I recognize His hand in the events of my life, I see how He stitches yet another square into the protective quilt He wraps me in.

Bearer of All Good, when things don't go according to plan, remind me to look through Your loving eyes to see the good You bring through it. Amen.
—Claire McGarry

GROWING IN FAITH

Is there something that isn't going right at the moment? See if you can look at the situation through Jesus's loving eyes and identify the good it may hold.

FINDING PURPOSE IN THE UGLY

For it is God who works in you to will and to act in order to fulfill his good purpose. —Philippians 2:13 (NIV)

November has arrived in my husband's and my native plant gardens. The hummingbirds have long gone. So have the robins and summer tanagers. The last of our fall bloomers—salvias, mistflowers, and asters—are winding down. In the morning, we wake to colder temperatures. Darkness falls earlier each evening.

As I walk our garden paths, I itch to trim the dead branches of our lantanas. Their leaves have dropped, and they litter the ground. Likewise, the Turk's caps, just a month ago so leafy green and tipped with red flowers, now stand nearly naked. I sigh when I pass the leggy branches of our rosinweed, bent to the ground, brown and dead. So ugly. They should be cut away.

But I refrain because, this winter, wild creatures will use these things. Beetles will burrow within dead stems. Insect pupae will hide in fallen leaves and survive there until they turn into moths, flies, and solitary bees in the spring. Among the brittle leaves, wrens and other birds will scavenge for those larvae. They'll find spiders and other insects to eat too.

I wish I could prune away the painful mistakes I've made. Guilt wracks my heart. But then our Creator comes, using what I see as unsightly for His good.

And, like our gardens when spring comes, I'm renewed once again.

Dear Lord, thank You for using what seems dead or flawed in me for Your glory. Amen.

—Sheryl Smith-Rodgers

GROWING IN FAITH

Today look at things that are past their prime in your garden. Ask God to feed, shelter, or otherwise help other living beings within them.

VARIETY IN THE GARDEN

He has made everything beautiful in its time.
—Ecclesiastes 3:11 (NKJV)

On my way out one morning, I spotted several small colorful bags on a shelf in the garage. I paused to pick one up and smiled. My husband had brought home these variety packs of tulip bulbs, a thoughtful gift since he knows tulips are my favorite.

This gift shifted my vision in a positive way. I had been planning to buy bulbs in carefully curated colors. I'd group them together and they'd be neat, tidy, and uniform in my flower beds. But here's the thing: Life is rarely neat or tidy. It's rarely orderly or uniform.

I've been leaning into the unknown, settling into not knowing what the next six months or year or even five years will hold. It's been freeing. Sometimes terrifying, but usually freeing.

God has been reminding me that He is the keeper of the variety of life's possibilities, and any ideas I have of how things ought to go or what I need to hold on to are falling away into peace and rest.

Today's verse says He makes all things beautiful in their time. We don't know what we're going to get, but His surprises bring unexpected beauty.

I'm grateful for the surprise bags of bulbs whose colors I can't predict. In fact, they're my new preference because variety symbolizes the best God has for us when we release our hopes and dreams into His care.

Thank You, God, for not revealing everything at once. I am grateful for the variety You create and for promising to make all things beautiful. Amen.
—Erin Keeley Marshall

GROWING IN FAITH

Buy a variety pack of seeds or bulbs.
Thank God for the surprises He brings.

DEATH ISN'T THE END

As for man, his days are like grass; he flourishes like a flower of the field; for the wind passes over it, and it is gone, and its place knows it no more.
—Psalm 103:15–16 (ESV)

A visit with my southern Granny always included a trip to a local farm to buy a watermelon. On the way, we drove past fields of cotton plants pregnant with swelling bolls.

"I wish I could grow cotton," I said. "But I doubt it would produce in Rhode Island. The season's too short."

Several months later, a lumpy envelope arrived in the mail. Inside was a package of cotton seeds. When the ground warmed, I planted the seeds in a sunny corner of the garden. They sprouted and grew into lush plants with pale pink flowers. When the flowers dropped off, small green bolls formed. I knew my cotton plants were racing the clock. *Would the bolls mature before the first frost killed them?*

Soon I heard the forecast I'd been dreading. I knew I couldn't save all the plants, but maybe I could save one. I dug up the biggest plant, potted it, and carried it inside. Within days, the leaves withered and turned brown. But before I could throw it away, an amazing thing happened—the dried-up bolls burst open. Inside was snowy white cotton and fuzzy seeds—enough for another attempt next year.

I often think of my cotton plant when seasons of life draw to a close. It reminds me that while the season may end, if I lived it for the Lord, the fruit it produced will remain and multiply.

Father, help me remember that every season ends, but the fruit of a life well-lived lasts for eternity. Amen.
—Lori Hatcher

GROWING IN FAITH

Today reflect on the changing seasons, outdoors and in you.

FALLOW GROUND

Sow for yourselves righteousness; reap steadfast love; break up your fallow ground, for it is the time to seek the LORD, that he may come and rain righteousness upon you. —Hosea 10:12 (ESV)

In recent weeks, I've attended a number of funerals. I've felt heavy with grief, withdrawn, and wanting only to numb my feelings. Even attending church has been painful because my emotions were so raw. Every praise song brought me to tears.

The ground of my life needed a little time to rest, to lie fallow. Soil can't produce nonstop. As I remembered the natural rhythm of the garden, I gave myself grace to withdraw for a time.

Then the day of a speaking engagement arrived. As weary and raw as I felt, I wondered if I could even form words or whether I'd burst into tears in the middle of teaching about writing. So, as Hosea urged, I sought the Lord. I poured out my sorrow, my fears, and my need for Him. I was willing to go where He sent me, but only if He was with me.

As I taught that night, God gently broke up the fallow ground within me. He planted new seeds in my heart, and I felt the fruit of His unfailing love as He provided strength. As difficult as it was to return to "normal life" after so much loss, I realized He was guiding me along the next step of healing.

The garden isn't meant to lie dormant for too long.

Dear Gardener of Our Hearts, pour Your unfailing love into our lives. Amen.

—Sharon Hinck

GROWING IN FAITH

Have you been withdrawing from God or from others recently? Ask the Lord to bring healing and prepare fallow ground for new seeds.

FINDING BEAUTY

One thing I ask from the LORD, this only do I seek: that I may dwell in the house of the LORD all the days of my life, to gaze on the beauty of the LORD and to seek him in his temple. —Psalm 27:4 (NIV)

As I looked through the rain-spattered window, my garden seemed to be only a mass of brown and gray. Everything was drooping and faded. The planting beds so recently overflowing with life and color were now covered in a mulch of brown leaves slowly beginning to decay. I tried reminding myself that as the leaves broke down they were adding nourishment to the soil to provide for next season's blossoms. However, I had trouble seeing ahead that far.

I decided I needed to purposefully search for something encouraging in my view. I stopped and looked at the garden again, determined to use a new set of eyes. I noticed there were still a few deeply crimson-colored leaves on the Japanese maple. Continuing my survey of the planting beds, I saw that the spent hydrangea blooms had aged to lovely bronze and sepia tones that would remain throughout the winter. I realized how beautiful the spent blooms would appear against the snow that was sure to arrive soon.

The abundant beauty of summer is easy for me to recognize. The new life of spring is an annual miracle. I have to look harder to see life and beauty in the early days of winter, but it is there for me to find.

Thank You, God, for new eyes that allow me to
find the beauty in each day. Amen.
—Chrystal Westbrook

GROWING IN FAITH

Ask the Lord to help you see the gifts of beauty He has provided for you today.

PEPPERED WITH FORGIVENESS

And do not forget to do good and share with others.
—Hebrews 13:16 (NIV)

In Texas, we have a native pepper plant called the chile pequin. Several of these bushes grow in my husband's and my native plant gardens. Last fall, they put out a plethora of pea-sized red peppers. Normally, mockingbirds gorge on the searing-hot fruit, but none showed up. Not wanting to waste the peppers, I asked local friends on social media if they'd like some.

"Yes, please," replied one neighbor right away.

Upon seeing her name, I frowned. Years ago, she'd been rude to me at a holiday party. I doubt she remembered, but I'd never forgotten. Had I forgiven her? Deep down, I knew I hadn't.

"Okay," I posted. "I'll pick some for you."

Bent over the chile bushes, I pulled one little pepper after another, dropping them into a plastic bowl. The repetitious motion soothed me as I thought of this woman and giving her the peppers. To my surprise, I realized I was smiling, not frowning. That long-held grudge just didn't matter anymore.

"Oh, thank you," she exclaimed, when she came by for the peppers. "I picked these for my father when I was little. He'd make a special sauce with them."

"You're so welcome," I said. "Let me know if you want more."

I waved as she drove away. Giving this person, for whom I'd so often had negative feelings, happiness had made *me* feel happy.

But, best of all, God had used those red-hot peppers to melt away my hurt over the past.

Thank You, Lord, for the joy that forgiveness brings. Amen.
—Sheryl Smith-Rodgers

GROWING IN FAITH

Share a gift or something from your garden with someone who has hurt or insulted you in the past. Forgive!

WINTER SUNRISE

Therefore we do not lose heart. Though outwardly we are wasting away, yet inwardly we are being renewed day by day. —2 Corinthians 4:16 (NIV)

Autumn is my least favorite season. While friends rave about the vibrant leaves as they change and the return of pumpkin spice lattes, sadness settles in my soul.

Summer is *my* season. Hot temperatures, lots of sunlight, yellow hibiscus, red begonias, and pink geraniums in full bloom. From April to October, I'm able to enjoy time outside in the pool or sitting on the back porch. I awake early and work from home in order to wrap up my workday by 4 p.m. and stay outside until dark. Every day feels like a celebration!

Last year, I took the passing of summer hard. I had a birthday that ended in a zero in mid-September. If my lifetime were divided into seasons, that birthday put me on the cusp of winter, the final season of my life. But I don't want summer to end. I don't want to grow older.

Logically, I know nothing I say or do can stop time. My vanity about aging cannot alter the seasons. That's why I'm in mourning.

On a December morning, I throw on a robe and take the dog outside. Daylight slowly illuminates the darkened sky. It grows into a fiery red-orange sunrise, the likes of which are never seen in my beloved summer. It's so magnificent that I snap a photo and post it on social media.

My emotional darkness brightens as I watch the sun rise in the sky. While different, this season has much to offer too.

Lord, please renew me physically, emotionally,
and spiritually in every season. Amen.
—Stephanie Thompson

GROWING IN FAITH

What is one thing about December
that you can celebrate today?

LESSONS FROM GARLIC

The LORD hath done great things for us; whereof we are glad.
—Psalm 126:3 (KJV)

In the Christmas movie *The Grinch,* garlic suffers a bad rap. The evil Grinch is said to have "garlic in his soul." Nutritionists' messages, though, are just the opposite. They tell us that garlic reduces the risk of various cancers and has strong antioxidant properties, among other things. And stepping into an Italian restaurant for a delicious dinner, you can smell the enticing, intoxicating aroma of garlic.

Personally, I love it so much that I planted a dozen cloves in my garden after consulting twenty or more videos of how to do so online.

"Aren't you kind of overdoing this?" my wife asked.

"No, we are going to be so healthy . . . maybe lonely, but healthy," I joked.

"I'm more concerned with our *spiritual* health, what seeds God is planting in our *souls,*" she said.

"Yes, you're right, dear, but are you okay with the garlic I planted this fall?" I asked. "I've waited all through the winter months thinking nothing was happening. Now the plants are six inches tall already."

Of course, I want spiritual growth. And garlic has spiritual lessons to teach. I've learned through this slow-growing garlic that God is working in my life even in the dark, cold winter of my experiences. Through rejection, persecution, health problems, and struggles, God is at work. Growth, marvelous newness has emerged. I look at the garlic growing and thank God that He is at work. There is a harvest of righteousness if I don't give up.

Garlic is good—and so is God!

Thank You, Lord, for working in my life. I won't give up. Amen.
—Durwood Smith

GROWING IN FAITH

Plant some garlic cloves in the fall. Thank God for His unceasing work.

Gardening is the art that uses flowers and plants as the paint and the soil and sky as the canvas.

ELIZABETH MURRAY, PROFESSIONAL GARDENER AND ARTIST

THE ART OF LIVING

Go, eat your bread with joy, And drink your wine with a merry heart; For God has already accepted your works. —Ecclesiastes 9:7 (NKJV)

"After I rake these leaves and put them in the compost," I said out loud, "then I need to put a load of clothes in the washer and give Ralph his medications, then I need to wrap a few presents and. . . ."

My to-do list looped and spun in my head like a broken record. Suddenly, a pair of squirrels playing a game of chase around the rosebush in the backyard garden caught my eye. They did somersaults and romped through the grass, then frolicked up the pecan tree and leapt branch to branch.

I laughed out loud. They're having fun, I thought to myself. When was the last time my husband, Ralph, and I had fun together? I couldn't remember.

Since I had become Ralph's caregiver, play was something that never looped and spun in my head. Fun was *never* on my endless to-do list, I realized.

Swish. Whoosh. The squirrels were back on the ground, rustling through leaves, searching for nuts to bury and store for their winter provisions. These busy little creatures were balancing work, play, and rest—the art of living was playing out right before my very eyes.

"Ralph," I said, after raking the leaves. "Want to work a puzzle together?"

He looked pleasantly surprised. "Yes! That would be fun," he said.

God, thank You for the gifts of play and enjoyment.
Remind me that these are also part of Your plan for my life.
—Shelly Niebuhr

GROWING IN FAITH

Give yourself permission to take a break from work today and enjoy something fun.

TETHERED TO ETERNITY

But the steadfast love of the LORD is from everlasting to everlasting.
—Psalm 103:17 (ESV)

December's chill bites, and I reach for the tightest-knit cap I can find. But I can't stifle the memory attached to this violet beanie. My dear friend Renee wore it the winter we traveled to Canada for her cancer treatment. A haunting thought follows: I'm one day closer to joining Renee in heaven.

I shouldn't fear, but I do. Endings are sad. Endings seem final.

Another tender memory descends, one that comforts. My Italian father-in-law plucking juicy grapes from the lush vines tethered to his fence for his grandkids. Facing winter, he would hard-prune those vines and then wait. His grapevines wouldn't die. They'd rest, then regenerate.

David the Psalmist understood this. He never put a period where God places a comma. In Psalm 103:15–19 (ESV), he followed "as for man, his days are like grass" with "But the steadfast love of the LORD is from everlasting to everlasting . . . The LORD has established His throne in the heavens, and his kingdom rules over all."

God's throne gleams beyond the heavens, transcending every beginning and ending I perceive. His regenerative power, my hope of eternity, runs over and under all my steps. Over every birth, every death, and every fear about tomorrow.

Like Grandpa George's grapevines in winter, what appears to be an end is, in truth, enduring. The knit hat that warmed Renee today warms me. And somehow, the everlasting comfort she's experiencing echoes across eternity to comfort me.

God, You're the Master Vinedresser! Thank You for tethering me securely to Your everlasting love. Amen.

—Kit Tosello

GROWING IN FAITH

Choose a vining indoor or outdoor plant. Meditate on the everlasting security of God as you tenderly tether it to a stake.

AN ENDURING PROMISE

"You heard me say, 'I am going away and I am coming back to you'."
—John 14:28 (NIV)

When I was eight years old, my mom presented me with a trowel and a flat of pansies. I planted them in a small triangular area near our side patio. Those little flowers brought much joy, with their mixed-color patterns and painted-on faces.

I didn't know then that pansies are among the oldest of cultivated flowers and that their name comes from the French word *pensée,* meaning "thought" or "remembrance." I just knew that they brought happiness.

The cheerful thought of pansies has since accompanied me every waning winter. The first flowers found at garden centers in spring and reappearing again in autumn, they are resilient and robust. Pansies are a hardy, happy flower. Pansies have edible qualities also and make a delightful garnish for cakes. Yet how many people trust them enough to take a bite?

A few weeks ago, in November, my last pansy of the season sat in its pot. It was a vibrant periwinkle color with a bright yellow center. The fragrance was pleasant as I lifted pansy to palate. I bit. Chewed. A sweet, unassuming flavor suggested constancy and comfort.

Pansies bid farewell to the growing season.

"We'll be back," they seem to say.

A sign of cheer at the first and an enduring promise at the last.

Through the winter, we anticipate their return.

Thank You, Jesus, for the happy pansy, which helps me to taste and see Your goodness. Thank You for Your promise to return again.

—Lisa Livezey

GROWING IN FAITH

Is there a young one who could benefit from the joy of planting pansies? In spring or fall, plan to present that person with a trowel and some pansies.

THE MINT GARDEN

But thanks be to God, who always leads us as captives in Christ's triumphal procession and uses us to spread the aroma of the knowledge of him everywhere. For we are to God the pleasing aroma of Christ among those who are being saved and those who are perishing.
—2 Corinthians 2:14–15 (NIV)

"I'm sick of trying to get the mower around that small area between the kitchen window and the driveway. Can you just *plant* something there?"

My husband, Jeff, was frustrated after struggling with that part of the lawn.

My brain began to swirl with the creative possibilities.

"Oh, yes," I said. "I'll plant an herb garden."

I grabbed my gardening books, measured the rectangular plot of land, bought a wide variety of herbs, and set off creating an herb garden. Cement blocks made the perfect edging. Once I filled it with soil, I planted oregano, basil, thyme, rosemary, cilantro, parsley, and mint.

That summer, the herb garden flourished. When walking past, I would rub my hands over the plants and smell the aroma that clung to my fingertips.

The next year, the mint came up and began to spread, gradually filling in the spots where other herbs had been. My herb garden turned into a fragrant mint garden.

Friends and family wonder why I let the mint continue to take over. I have a good reason: its sweet aroma reminds me of my grandmother's yard, and I love a cup of hot tea made from fresh mint leaves. Most of all, though, my husband loves not having to mow there!

Jesus, may others smell Your aroma coming from me.
—Beth Gormong

GROWING IN FAITH

Drink a cup of coffee, hot tea, or hot chocolate, and thank God that He uses you to spread His "aroma."

A GARDEN OF MEMORIES

"For I will pour water on the thirsty land, and streams on the dry ground; I will pour out my Spirit on your offspring, and my blessing on your descendants."—Isaiah 44:3 (NIV)

A patch of land in the far corner of our backyard appears to be nothing but rocky red dirt. But, today, on the anniversary of my dad's death, I see a garden blooming with memories.

Dad visited me more often after his cancer diagnosis. We would sit on the deck in the Adirondack chairs he made for my husband and me for Christmas one year. Once, Dad pointed at the desolate patch and said it would be a great place for a vegetable garden.

"I've always wanted to plant tomatoes like you used to do," I replied. "But I don't even know where to start."

When he offered to help, I worried that it would be too much for him. He tired easily those days, but he never complained. This made it difficult to know when he had reached his limit. He promised me that he wouldn't do more than he could handle.

We spent several weeks attempting to till the ground with no success. However, as we worked, we laughed, cried, and shared memories.

We finally gave up. That Oklahoma red clay was more stubborn than we were.

Dad is gone. But as I look at that patch, I don't see dirt. I imagine a garden bed, blooming with memories to pass down to our loved ones.

Father, thank You for the precious memories our loved ones leave behind to share with our future generations.

—Kristy Dewberry

GROWING IN FAITH

Look with imagination at an area of your life that seems desolate. What might God be growing there?

TEARS IN HIS BOTTLE

You number my wanderings; Put my tears into Your bottle; Are they not in Your book? —Psalm 56:8 (NKJV)

Today is cut-back day. About every six months, I trim my houseplants back. I own a lot of plants, including a large pothos ivy that flourishes in my walk-in shower. I always hesitate to make that first cut to one of its long vines. My schefflera grows fast and must be trimmed more often just so we can get around the dining room table.

My plants always seem healthier a few days after their trimming. No matter how bad it might feel to me, cutting them back keeps my plants strong. I've always had a green thumb when it comes to indoor plants. People often ask me if I talk to them. I don't. Well, not usually, but I do gently pat their leaves as I walk past.

I wonder if it's hard on God when the time comes that He must trim us back. I think it probably is. I do know, as the Psalmist says, God collects our tears in His bottle.

As an expression of love in Bible times, each mourner at a funeral placed one of their tears in a bottle, then presented the bottle to the family or buried it with the deceased. What a loving gesture! I wish we still did that today.

God corrects, redirects, and trims us because He loves us. And when we cry or grieve, He grieves with us, saving our tears.

Lord, help me to be aware of Your presence when I am hurting. Thank You for Your compassionate love. Amen.

—Pamela Haskin

GROWING IN FAITH

Think of someone you love who is in a season of being "trimmed back." How can you offer love to them today?

PLANTING SEEDS

Very truly I tell you, unless a kernel of wheat falls to the ground and dies, it remains only a single seed. But if it dies, it produces many seeds.
—John 12:24 (NIV)

Because I have an active imagination, I often have big aspirations. There's nothing wrong with setting goals or dreaming of ways I can make a big difference, but sometimes I can get so attached to *my* ideas that I stop listening for *my Shepherd's* leading.

Years ago, I led a Christian arts organization. When difficulties arose, I stubbornly plowed ahead, causing stress to those around me and terrible pressure on myself. I had latched on to my vision with such narrow focus that I didn't even consider that God was steering me in a new direction.

Finally, I stepped back. God knew that I needed to release insisting on doing things *my* way. I had to release *my* concept of "success."

Like a seed crushed and buried, I wondered if God was done with me. Instead, over time, He led me toward writing novels and devotions. With every publication, He is able to grow something new and spread the reach of His message, but only when the hard shell of following Him *my* way is broken apart and discarded.

As a friend told me, we may feel *buried*, but we are actually *planted*.

Again today, I prayed about my activities and asked if it was time for me to lay anything down so He can resurrect something far better in and through me.

Lord, show us when to release our plans and reassure us of the new seeds You will produce in us. Amen.
—Sharon Hinck

GROWING IN FAITH

Today ask God to guide you. Trust Him to plant new seeds within you.

GARDEN AT REST

"All people are like grass, and all their glory is like the flowers of the field; the grass withers and the flowers fall." —1 Peter 1:24 (NIV)

The days are getting shorter, and the nights are cool. The garden responds with a kind of transformative magic that signals it is time for rest. God reminds us of a repetition of the seasons but promises to return the garden, dressed in her emerald splendor, painted with the endless color combinations in His palette.

Nearby is the dusty blush of the nannyberry and the fiery scarlet leaves of the burning bush. The bare vines of the clematis cling to the trellis, dried and lifeless. The centerpiece—the grand Dragon Wing begonia—still hangs onto her flagship red blossoms that she graced us with all summer, but her leaves are shriveling and edged in brown. The stalks of the peonies, irises, lilies, and lavender are erect but dried. A few tough daisies assert an effort for another blooming spree. Petite purple blossoms of the loosestrife have faded, her showy foliage turned a dusty silver-gray.

Once a peaceful, stunning place, with bouquets of blossoms in every size and hue, the garden is now changed, withered and drawn inside the surround of its weathered pickets. Earthy animals await their sleep under snow.

The area is a sure reminder that God leads us through the seasons He has planned, both for us *and* for our gardens. Winter is a season for all to rest and renew. While the plants grow deeper roots, we, too, have opportunity to deepen our roots in faith.

Heavenly Father, thank You for the lessons of our gardens.

—Cookie Cranston

GROWING IN FAITH

Winter is a perfect time to slow down.
Today reflect on how you can rest this season.

CHRISTMASTIME POPCORN

The land yields its harvest; God, our God, blesses us. —Psalm 67:6 (NIV)

A few years ago, my two brothers, Timothy and William, and my husband worked together to plant a family garden on William's farm. The three men planted corn, peas, potatoes, squash, and butter beans. More recently, Timothy decided to plant corn for popping, just for fun. Sadly, when he was just forty-seven years old, Timothy tragically died.

All of us have grieved mightily.

At Christmastime last year, William surprised my family and me with jars of corn kernels.

Through tears, he said, "This gift is from Timothy. It's some of the popcorn he helped plant and harvest last year. I'd saved a lot for seeds, so we can use it to make popcorn. That way, we all can enjoy memories of Timothy and be reminded of how much he loved the garden . . . and all of us."

William said he plans to plant some of the seeds again this coming year for another crop of Timothy's popcorn. As William said, "Each year, Timothy will contribute to the family garden as well as to our fun at Christmastime."

What a precious way to remember my brother every year!

Thank You, God, for family and for memories. Be with all who grieve the loss of someone they love. Bring us comfort and joy, Lord. Amen.

—Julie Lavender

GROWING IN FAITH

Tonight pop some popcorn and share a bowl with your family. While snacking, talk about favorite family memories. End your time together with prayer, giving thanks for each family member.

NEIGHBORS PLANTING KINDNESS

Each of us should please our neighbors for their good, to build them up.
—Romans 15:2 (NIV)

Early one fall, my family and I moved from a warmer climate to a colder one, farther north. Weeks later, on a frigid winter morning, our new neighbors rang the doorbell to let us know that there were icicles on the side of our house. When we went to inspect them, we discovered that our sprinkler system had burst. Those icicles were due to frozen water lines. In our previous home, we had never closed our sprinkler system for the winter, so this was new to us. We'd simply gardened using the sprinkler system year-round.

We thanked the kind neighbors, and they offered us the name of a reputable sprinkler system service. The repairmen arrived and quickly replaced a cracked valve.

Before they left, our neighbors also explained that we were now in a different gardening zone. That small difference in zones meant that not only would we need to winterize our sprinkler system but also we'd plant different flowers, grass, and plants than we had at the old place. We made careful note of these things.

In the spring, we opened the sprinkler system as instructed. We discussed what plants would work in our new gardening zone. And when late fall rolled around, we were prepared for those freezing temperatures.

Just about then, new neighbors moved in from out of state to a house across the cul-de-sac from us. We told them our story of the frozen lines, and we shared the zone difference with them as well. Neighbors have to keep neighbors prepared!

Lord, thank You for bringing kind and helpful neighbors into our lives. Amen.
—Amy Barnes

GROWING IN FAITH

Reflect on how you can better prepare for new "zones" in your life.

Gardening is all about optimism. I put a seed in the ground. I consistently tend it, confident I will see the results, in time, of the nurture I have provided.

MARY ANNE RADMACHER, AUTHOR

STOP WHILE YOU STILL HAVE JOY!

"The joy of the LORD is your strength." —Nehemiah 8:10 (NIV)

If you work with kids in the garden, you will discover that they are full of joy. Discovering an earthworm or pulling fresh carrots from the ground can produce squeals of excitement. We adults take delight in these things, too, but often more in the accomplishment of our days' work. It is our job to help guide and direct our children's focus so the enjoyment of the things around them is balanced with focus, perseverance, and faithfulness. Unfortunately, in trying to do so, we can unintentionally steal the joy from our kids' experience, and many grow up to hate the idea of gardening.

An African friend of mine grew up being made to work in large, weedy cornfields where he felt discouraged and burnt out at the end of each day. But later he discovered a secret that has led him to love having his own small farm.

"Always stop while you still have joy," he told me.

By not waiting until the last minute and managing his time where he can stop while still wanting more, he's found a new love for gardening.

We all need to maintain our joy even as we work to overcome our laziness and distraction. But let's monitor our joy levels so we don't burn out.

Lord, please show me how to walk humbly with You as I work, being willing to acknowledge when I need to stop and come back to a task tomorrow.

—Noah Sanders

GROWING IN FAITH

Whatever you do today, monitor your joy level. If you find it lacking, evaluate whether you are trying to bite off more than God has given you the resources for.

BEAUTY REVEALED

He grew up before him like a tender shoot, and like a root out of dry ground. He had no beauty or majesty to attract us to him, nothing in his appearance that we should desire him. —Isaiah 53:2 (NIV)

A mild Alabama winter allowed my biologist brother, Jeff, and me to continue our nature exploration of the family farm. The ATV bounced across "the bottoms," an open area that stretched for several acres at the base of the bluff. We stopped for a hike when we reached the edge of the woods.

"Look at these purple berries," I said. "They glitter like pearls."

"That's a beautyberry shrub," Jeff said. "I'm surprised the deer haven't eaten all the berries by now."

In spring and early summer, the beautyberry plant blends into the landscape, its small flowers barely visible from a distance. But in late summer and fall, a transformation takes place. Clusters of berries encircle the stems and ripen to a vibrant, shimmery purple. The berries last until winter, providing food for deer, songbirds, raccoons, and other animals.

Jesus's earthly appearance was somewhat ordinary, too, at the beginning. The people in His hometown knew Him as a carpenter, Mary's son, and the brother of James, Joseph, Judas, and Simon. When the right season arrived, however, Jesus revealed His beauty and majesty.

He paid the ultimate price, defeated death, and set into motion God's plan of redemption that offers us eternal life today.

Beautiful Jesus, I bow my head and bend my knees in gratitude for Your great sacrifice.
—Becky Alexander

GROWING IN FAITH

Do you view yourself as ordinary, blending with the world around you? Imagine how Jesus could touch the lives of others through you. Ask Him to help you display His beauty today.

NEW FRUIT

"This is to my Father's glory, that you bear much fruit, showing yourselves to be my disciples."—John 15:8 (NIV)

My husband and I have begun a new gardening venture. Near the back of our property, we set wooden stakes in the ground and ran rows of wire from post to post. Next spring, blackberry branches, called canes, will climb up and along the wires. Our first harvest will be small, but once the bushes are well established, we anticipate a bounty of blackberries.

Guiding us on this venture is Bill, a man of God who gave us starts from his own plants. "When you mess it all up," he says, "call me and I'll come fix it." His humor is a bonus as we learn.

The most important lesson Bill taught us is to prune our blackberries. Once a cane produces fruit, it will not produce again. Old canes must be cut off so new berry-producing canes can grow. Like these bushes, sometimes ministries need to be cut so new fruit can be produced.

I learned this years ago. We started a young married Sunday school class that flourished—until church leadership decided to cut Sunday school for adults. They wanted us to meet in small groups in homes. I wasn't thrilled. We'd invested so much in our class!

Soon I realized people who turned down a church invite would accept an invitation to someone's home. Many eventually came to church. So many, in fact, that our church opened a second campus.

Cutting a once-fruitful branch was difficult, but, oh, the new fruit we produced for God's glory!

Father, I want to bear much fruit for You. Amen.

—Karen Sargent

GROWING IN FAITH

Is old fruit preventing you from flourishing?
Cut it. Try something new and watch it grow.

GREAT-GRANDMOTHER AND GREAT GARDENING

I am reminded of your sincere faith, which first lived in your grandmother Lois and in your mother Eunice and, I am persuaded, now lives in you also. —2 Timothy 1:5 (NIV)

There's a small ceramic statue in my china cabinet of a grandmother and child gardening together on their knees. The grandmother is bent over the child, holding a watering can. At first glance, it's only a statue, but the memories from that statue are far more important. I remember precious moments with my great-grandmother as much as I remember dirt under my fingernails and overwatering seeds.

When we gardened together, I was mainly the seed placer and watering can navigator. Whenever I visited her house, she and I headed to our special spot in the garden. We examined the progress of the seeds and watered them together. She talked to me about making the soil more helpful for plant growth. She explained how plants need water and food just as people do. I not only learned how seeds become plants but also learned about her faith as we gardened on our knees, praying for the seeds.

One Christmas right before she died, my great-grandmother gifted me the statue. I've brought it along with me all through life, moving it from house to house as a remembrance of her. Our time together was a blessing and, even though I can no longer kneel with her to plant flowers, those early gardening sessions have guided the course of my life.

Lord, thank You for the grandparents and elders You've placed in our lives. We are grateful for their powerful witness. Amen.

—Amy Barnes

GROWING IN FAITH

Even the smallest seeds, smallest children, and smallest acts can create growth and faith. How can you share God's love with a little one this week?

THE BEST CHRISTMAS GIFT EVER

For God so loved the world that he gave his one and only Son, that whoever believes in him shall not perish but have eternal life. —John 3:16 (NIV)

"Open this one!" My husband beamed with excitement.

I shook the box. *What could it be?* Whatever it was, it was very light. I ripped into the wrapping and opened the lid to see a folded piece of paper. I looked around the room, my confusion tinged with excitement. I saw the big smile on my husband's face and knew this would be a good gift. *But what could it be?* I unfolded the paper to see a photo of a beautiful orange garden tiller. I had wanted one for years!

It was the best Christmas gift I've ever received—that tiller has become my favorite part of gardening. I love the feel of the handle shaking as the tiller lifts and turns clods of dirt, ripping out weeds and preparing the soil. When I use the loud behemoth of a machine, I feel strong, like I have superhuman powers. All I need to do is steer as it moves effortlessly down the rows, quickly turning the weed-covered garden into a carpet of beautiful brown soil.

I'm thankful God weeds my life with His tiller-like strength. I'm thankful He is willing to work in my sin-infested life, pulling out weeds that want to starve my roots and planting His spirit in my soul.

Jesus, thank You for forgiving us of our sins, for making us clean so that You can plant the fruits of the Spirit in our lives.

—Beth Gormong

GROWING IN FAITH

What "weeds" are growing in your life? Ask God today to pull them out so that you can produce healthy fruit.

A TREE THAT ENDURES

He plants a pine, and the rain nourishes it. —Isaiah 44:14 (NKJV)

My family moved into a newly built house when I was twelve years old. The yard was bare. Not a tree or shrub or even a flower grew in it. My dad sowed grass seed and put in bushes. My mom planted flower bulbs. But the big fix happened at Christmas.

"We're going to have a living tree this year instead of a cut one," my parents announced to my siblings and me. "A tree to help us remember this Christmas even after it's over."

So into our family room came a six-foot-tall "balled" pine tree. Its wonderful scent filled the house. We decorated it with fat multicolored lights and, after the ornaments and treetop angel were in place, draped icicle tinsel over every branch. It was the prettiest Christmas tree ever.

That January, my dad planted the tree in the wide swath of ground between our driveway and the road. That healthy, happy pine tree seemed to grow before our very eyes and smiled on us every time we walked out the front door. Decades passed. We kids grew up and moved away. Our parents grew old and went on to their heavenly reward.

One December, my siblings and I sold the house and gathered to turn the keys over to the new owners. Although it was far too tall to hang ornaments from, we stood beneath our beloved tree and tossed handfuls of icicle tinsel over the lower branches.

We knew that Mother and Daddy were celebrating the sacred season with us.

Lord, we thank You for sweet memories.

—Jennie Ivey

GROWING IN FAITH

What are your favorite childhood memories?
Share them with a member of your family or a friend.

HUMBLY ROOTED

Let us not become weary in doing good, for at the proper time we will reap a harvest if we do not give up. —Galatians 6:9 (NIV)

This morning, the philodendron slip cascading from a too-small glass bottle in our bay window causes me shame. I had every intention of someday potting it in soil. Yet now the vase is so stuffed with a thriving root system, I'd have a tough time extracting it from the narrow-necked bottle. *Why haven't I potted it yet?*

I know very well why. Because it takes me back to the yellow-tiled kitchen of my childhood home, where my mother usually kept something rooting on the sill. Often it was a glossy avocado pit or a sweet potato suspended with toothpicks over a mason jar. She took joy from this simple act, while her life held adult-sized struggles I often knew nothing about. Struggles forging a heart of empathy and kindness.

Decades later, as a widow and shut-in using an oxygen tank, Mom questioned her usefulness. But I knew better. I knew of lonely folks sustained by her phone calls. At her memorial, I watched a burly oxygen-delivery guy shed tears of gratitude for her encouragement. And today I see how her million tiny kindnesses nurtured my own compassion and my children's.

Like Mom, I'm tempted to think of my life as unremarkable. But this flourishing philodendron slip and Galatians 6:9 remind me that patient endurance and other-centered love, like my mom's, are the humble roots of a holy harvest.

Lord, help me to persevere, honoring the high value You place on doing, with great love, things that appear insignificant.

—Kit Tosello

GROWING IN FAITH

Reflect with gratitude on someone whose seemingly unremarkable life of faithfulness left a good mark on you.

A PLUM-PERFECT PLAN

"The LORD himself goes before you and will be with you; he will never leave you nor forsake you. Do not be afraid; do not be discouraged."
—Deuteronomy 31:8 (NIV)

Very soon, my childhood home will be torn down. The one-hundred-year-old farmhouse will be demolished and most of the land surrounding it will be cleared to make way for a new commercial real estate development.

I'm struggling with this loss, and I asked my husband to take one last walk on the property with me. The woods are overgrown; the fields are filled with briars and brambles, and the paths my siblings and I once walked as kids are marred with fallen trees.

Just before we got back to the old homeplace, my husband and I spotted one of the plum trees that faithfully produced delicious pink plums when I was a child. They'd stopped producing fruit a long time ago, but I remembered picking the fruit as a family to make plum jelly.

The homemade treat tasted best on warm, buttered toast, and it often accompanied eggs and grits for breakfast. Yum! I can still recall the taste now after all these years!

I'm not sure what the future plans hold for my old stomping ground, but what I am sure of is this: God not only knows those plans but also will walk with me each step of the way.

That's an assurance I can count on, and it's a plum-perfect plan.

Dear God, when I'm facing uncertainty and change, help me remember that You go before me and behind me and You promise to never leave me. Amen.
—Julie Lavender

GROWING IN FAITH

Today taste a spoonful of jam and reflect on the sweetness of God's grace.

GOD'S PLAN

Your eyes saw my unformed body; all the days ordained for me were written in your book before one of them came to be. —Psalm 139:16 (NIV)

My mom is eighty-eight years old. She has no interest in eating or drinking, and hospice is involved in her care due to her recent weight loss. She is confined to her bed or recliner. She doesn't know my sisters and me anymore, although we visit frequently. And today I learned that she has pneumonia.

I don't know how or what to pray as I sit, bundled up, on my deck and watch the snow fall. It is gently blanketing the winter remnants of my garden. Mom's quality of life is poor, but is she ready for her life on earth to end? I don't know.

I find myself contemplating God's creation of flowers. What a beautiful plan He designed, with annuals completing their life cycles in one season and perennials returning year after year.

Our lives on earth are like flowering plants. When we complete our life cycle, our seeds—our souls—remain, ready to sprout again in heaven. Once we get to heaven, our life cycle never ends.

I don't know God's plan for the remainder of Mom's earthly life cycle. And I still don't know how or what to pray for Mom, but it doesn't matter. God knows the plan.

Thank You, Father, for the assurance that Your plans for us are perfect.
—Kristy Dewberry

GROWING IN FAITH

Today, when you pray, try to imagine the cycles of your life and recognize that God is working out His plan for you.

A CONTINUOUS WORK

He who began a good work in you will carry it on to completion until the day of Christ Jesus. —Philippians 1:6 (NIV)

A dark-eyed junco flits from the white poplar branch to the pine below. Towhees call from the lilac bushes, their flashy orange bellies glinting in Colorado's December sunshine. Two weeks ago, we bid farewell to our first pollinator garden. We packed up and moved to this half-acre of land nestled up against the foothills. It sits on a lake, and the first time we drove here, a chorus of bird calls greeted us. Deep inside myself, I knew we were home.

Although it was difficult to leave our native pollinator garden, I trust we did something eternal there. Separated by only a few miles, what we began there will connect with our work here, when we break ground this spring. Our new pollinator garden, bursting at the seams of my imagination, will be an extension of the living corridor system we started at our prior home.

An eagle circles above the lake. Bull elk—five of them—wander down the street, stopping to nibble at late-season apples. God is constantly doing these gracious acts of connection in my spirit just like our corridor gardens. His work is a consistent cadence in my soul. He is not a God of loose ends. Instead, He utilizes every step of the journey to grow me right where I'm planted.

Lord, help me see all the interconnections and relations
in the work You are carrying out in my life.
—Eryn Lynum

GROWING IN FAITH

Look back over this past year. Consider what connections God made for you. What people or opportunities did He bring into your life to help you grow?

About the Authors

Michelle Medlock Adams is a best-selling author of more than 100 books, including *Dinosaur Devotions, The Christmas Devotional,* and *Dachshund Through the Snow.* She is also a *New York Times* best-selling ghostwriter and has won more than 80 industry awards, including an ECPA Gold Medallion for *Our God Is Bigger Than That!* Michelle is married to her high school sweetheart, Jeff, and they have two married daughters, six adorable grandchildren, and three spoiled miniature dachshunds.

Becky Alexander loves to write about colorful wildflowers and singing warblers on her family's farm in Decatur, Alabama. Her biologist brother and teacher sister helped her create *Clover's Wildflower Field Trip*, a paperback picture book that supports elementary science units on plants and natural habitats. Her work also appears in Guideposts' *Mornings with Jesus*, *Pray a Word a Day*, and *Too Amazing for Coincidence*. Send Becky a message and find all her books at happychairbooks.com.

Amy Barnes is an editor and writer who has written for a wide range of publications, including *Parabola*, *Motherly*, *Allrecipes*, *Southern Living*, and Guideposts' *Strength & Grace* devotional magazine. Her third collection of short stories, *Child Craft,* was published by Belle Point Press in 2023.

Jeannie Blackmer is an author who lives in Boulder, Colorado, with her husband, Zane. Her most recent books include *Talking to Jesus: A Fresh Perspective on Prayer* and *MomSense: A Common-Sense Guide to Confident Mothering.* She's passionate about using written words to inspire hope in women and encourage growth in their relationships with Jesus. Find out more about Jeannie at jeannieblackmer.com.

Cathy Bryant is an author whose heart's desire is to share faith in God with others through her writing. In addition to her devotionals and Bible studies, she enjoys penning fictional stories of God's life-changing grace in the *Miller's Creek* series of novels. *Texas Roads,* the first book in the series, was a finalist in the 2009 American Christian Fiction Writers' Genesis contest. She has also penned Christmas novellas, all with faith-based themes.

Tamara Bundy is a children's book author as well as the author of several nonfiction inspirational books. A former columnist for *The Cincinnati Post*, she currently teaches English and creative writing at Miami University. Tamara inspires thousands with her talks throughout the country. You can follow her on most social media platforms as well as her website: tamarabundy.com

Isabella Campolattaro admits to loving plants more than gardening itself. She is a longtime contributor to *Mornings with Jesus* and many other Guideposts books. An active ghostwriter, blogger, speaker, and retreat leader, Isabella is the author of *Embracing Life: Letting God Determine Your Destiny.* With an MS in public relations and management, she formerly worked in corporate communications. Isabella and her two sons enjoy life on Florida's lush Suncoast. Connect with her at isabellacampolattaro.com.

Sabra Ciancanelli is a writer and editor living in upstate New York. She holds an MFA in writing and has authored two books, hundreds of articles, and more than 1,000 devotions for *60 Days of Prayer, Daily Guideposts,* and *Walking in Grace.* Her passion is helping others recognize God's love and divine guidance so that they experience extraordinary blessings in their everyday lives.

Linda S. Clare is the award-winning author of eight books, including *The Fence My Father Built* and *Thank God for Cats!* (Broadstreet, 2023). She also works as a writing coach and teacher. She lives, writes, and gardens in the Pacific Northwest, where God's beauty and natural wonders often astound her. She writes a weekly column, The Deep End, at lindasclare.substack.com, writes free weekly writing tips at lindasclare.com, and loves connecting with readers @lindasclare on Facebook or Instagram.

Ben Cooper is a husband, father, author, speaker, and beekeeper. He grew up on a family farm and graduated from Penn State. Ben worked as an agricultural specialist for Maryland. He and his wife live in southern Pennsylvania. His books include *All Nature Sings* and a children's picture book series called *Created Critters.* He has been writing for *All God's Creatures* since 2023. Ben enjoys speaking and writing about God's wonderful creation. Connect with Ben at cooperville@breezeline.net.

Cookie Cranston went home to the Lord prior to this book being published. She worked at her local high school's library for thirty-two years. She had a passion for literature, publishing a number of books as well as contributing stories and devotions to various Guideposts publications. We are grateful for her many contributions.

Jessi Creed is a homeschool teacher, successful business consultant, and first-time Guideposts author. Her greatest achievements are the three precious treasures that call her Mommy and enjoying life with her soulmate. Native to the Blue Ridge Mountains, her hobbies include bird-watching, exploring nature, gardening, reading, and cruising.

About the Authors

Kristy Dewberry is a freelance writer. She was chosen as a winner of the Guideposts Workshop Contest in 2020 and recognized by *Guideposts* magazine as one of five women to celebrate on International Women's Day. She is a contributing writer to *Strength & Grace* and many other publications. When not writing, Kristy runs her eBay business and travels with her husband. She has six brilliant grandchildren, a faithful dog with separation anxiety, and a cranky parrot.

Walking in Grace writer **Shawnelle Eliasen** and her husband, Lonny, live near the banks of the Mississippi River in LeClaire, Iowa. They have five sons, four of them now in college or beyond. Although she has had to adjust to many changes around letting her boys go to live independently, she has found peace and contentment in her new life. Most important, she says, is our salvation and the new life Jesus gave when He released us from our sin sentence.

Candee Fick is an award-winning author of Christian romance novels and inspirational devotionals. She is also the wife of a high school football coach and the mother of three children, including a daughter with a rare genetic syndrome. When not busy weaving intricate plotlines at her favorite coffee shop, she can be found exploring the great Colorado outdoors, indulging in dark chocolate, or savoring happily-ever-after endings through a good book.

Julie Fisk—a farmer's daughter and licensed attorney—loves spending time in God's presence as she tends her Minnesota garden. A coauthor of several devotionals, including *One Year Daily Acts of Gratitude*, Julie shares stories of God's faithfulness through writing, speaking, and her online community, The Ruth Experience. Connect with Julie and her coauthors for encouragement, resources, and faith-filled community on social media or through their monthly newsletter.

Beth Gormong is a co-author of three devotional collections, *Hello, Beautiful!; Yes, You Can!;* and *Growing the Fruit of the Spirit.* She regularly contributes to Guidepost's *Strength & Grace* magazine and Guideposts books such as *Evenings with Jesus, Pray a Word a Day, Volume 2,* and *God's Constant Presence.* She seeks to encourage others to see truth and beauty. You can find her at bgormong.com and GreenGableStudio Etsy shop.

Lynne Hartke explores desert trails with her husband, Kevin, in Chandler, Arizona, where they are on staff at a church and where Kevin is the mayor. A breast cancer survivor, Lynne was named a Voice of Hope with the American Cancer Society in 2018. Lynne is the author of *Under a Desert Sky* and a monthly *WonderFULL* newsletter.

The couple has four grown children and four grandchildren. Connect with her at lynnehartkeauthor.com.

Pamela Haskin is an authority on wilderness survival. She is the author of the award-winning book *A Deliberate Life: A Journey into the Alaskan Wilderness* about her many years on a remote Alaskan homestead. After twenty-two years in Alaska, she and her husband of forty-six years, Jeff, moved to Sulphur Springs, Texas, where they are enjoying retirement. Pamela also creates paper illustrations and cards as a paper artist. She has been writing for Guideposts publications for twenty-nine years and loves sharing her faith through her words and artwork. Connect with her at pamelahaskin.com.

Lori Hatcher is a transplanted Yankee living happily in the South. Although she's delivered newspapers in a blizzard, she prefers to write transformational devotions from a sunny beach or a mountain cabin. The author of six devotionals with Our Daily Bread Publishing, including *Think on These Things: 60 Thoughtful Devotions for Renewed Peace,* Lori loves helping busy people connect with God in meaningful ways. Connect with Lori on her blog, *Refresh,* at lorihatcher.com.

Sharon Hinck is an aspirational gardener who imagines living off the land but really grows only enough vegetables for a few salads. She loves seeing God's creativity in the beauty of flowers and plants, and that theme shows up in many of her award-winning novels. Stop by to chat about your garden at her website, sharonhinck.com.

Jennie Ivey lives and writes in Tennessee. She attended the Guideposts Writers Workshop in 2008 and has written for many Guideposts publications. She's a weekly columnist for her hometown newspaper, the *Cookeville Herald-Citizen*, and is the author of three books, two about Tennessee history and one about Elvis. Jennie is the mother of three grown children and "Marmie" to the six cutest grandkids in the world. In addition to growing things, she enjoys reading, hiking, horseback riding, and bicycle riding, as well as hanging out with family and friends. Visit her at jennieivey.com.

Heather Jepsen is the pastor at First Presbyterian Church in Warrensburg, Missouri. She has been serving small churches for twenty years. She and her husband, Lars, have two kids, Olivia and Henry, as well as a wide variety of pets. They have practiced gardening in California, Washington, and Missouri. When she is not pastoring, gardening, or writing, Heather likes to quilt and play the harp. Heather also writes for Guideposts' *Strength & Grace* magazine, *All God's Creatures, Mornings with Jesus,* and other volumes. Read more at pastorheatherjepsen.com.

About the Authors

Julie Lavender is the author of *A Gingerbread House, Children's Bible Stories for Bedtime, Strength for All Seasons: A Mom's Devotional of Powerful Verses and Prayers,* and *365 Ways to Love Your Child.* Together with her husband, she writes educational books for kids, combining his wildlife biology and entomology experiences and her education and teaching experiences. They are the authors of *Raising Good Sons.* Julie and David love visiting their four kids, two sons-in-love, and three grandchildren.

Jeanette Levellie's relationship with Jesus and her family are the center of her heart. She has one husband, two grown kids, three grandchildren, and several spoiled-rotten cats. She lives in Paris, Illinois. Jeanette is the author of six books and hundreds of articles, sharing her experiences (and hilarious mishaps) of walking with Jesus. Jeanette's hobbies include gardening, watching old movies, and reading novels to escape housework. Find her musings at jeanettelevellie.com, Facebook, and X.

Lisa Livezey is a faith-filled devotional writer and blogger from the Philly suburbs. She is the author of *Minding Mom: A Caregiver's Devotional Story,* written to encourage caregivers. Her weekly photo devotions are viewed worldwide and utilized by Visio Divina prayer groups. Lisa serves on the executive team at Heart of the Father Ministries and sometimes on summer weekends can be spotted sailing the Chesapeake Bay alongside her husband. Visit Lisa online at lisalivezey.com.

Eryn Lynum is a certified Master Naturalist and hosts the *Nat Theo: Nature Lessons Rooted in the Bible* podcast. She is author of *The Nature of Rest: What the Bible and Creation Teach Us About Sabbath Living, Rooted in Wonder: Nurturing Your Family's Faith Through God's Creation,* and *936 Pennies.* She lives in Colorado with her husband, Grayson, and their four children. Eryn has been featured on broadcasts including Focus on the Family and FamilyLife Today.

Erin Keeley Marshall has enjoyed writing for Guideposts books for many years and counts those opportunities among her favorite career blessings. Her work spans numerous genres as a writer and an editor, and she is published in both fiction and nonfiction. Visit her at erinkeeleymarshall.com, on Facebook at Erin Keeley Marshall, Author, and on Instagram @erinkeeleymarshall.

Claire McGarry is a maker of lists, mistakes, brownies, and soups. Author of *Grace in Tension: Discover Peace with Martha and Mary* and the family Lenten devotionals *Abundant Mercy* and *With Our Savior,* she regularly contributes to *Living Faith* and *Mornings with Jesus.* Residing in New Hampshire with her husband and three kids, she would love to connect via her Facebook Author page and/or her blog *ShiftingMyPerspective.*

Shelly Niebuhr is a retired Certified Music Practitioner and has a master's degree in counseling/education. She worked as a musician in various healthcare settings for twenty years, visiting diverse patient populations from age sixteen to one hundred in hospitals, nursing homes, assisted-living facilities, hospice, memory care, and rehabilitation hospitals. In March 2020, she became a full-time caregiver for her husband. Shelly grew up on a pecan tree farm in central Texas, where she learned to love and appreciate the natural world. She now lives near Dallas with her husband and two cats.

Shirley Raye Redmond's writing has appeared in multiple Guideposts devotionals as well as three Guideposts mystery series. Her children's book *Courageous World Changers: 50 True Stories of Daring Women of God* (Harvest House) won the 2021 Christianity Today Book Award in its category. She has been married for fifty years to her college sweetheart. They live in northern New Mexico. Touch base via Facebook or through her website at shirleyrayeredmond.com.

Cynthia Ruchti has spent most of her adult life engaged in writing projects—magazine articles, devotions, newspaper columns, scripts for a long-running radio broadcast, and inspirational novels and nonfiction. She delights in exploring the intersection of our stories and God's story. She's also passionate about helping others gain the confidence to say, "I can't unravel. I'm hemmed in Hope." Cynthia and her husband live in Wisconsin near their three children and seven grandchildren. She serves on her church's worship team and enjoys photographing hints of God's glory in the world around us.

Emily E. Ryan is a minister's wife, mother of four, and junior high English teacher who cannot be trusted with houseplants. Inspired by *The Secret Garden*, she now sees God's fingerprints in every petal, leaf, and thorn. A writer and speaker for over twenty years, her work appears in *Mornings with Jesus* and other devotionals, and her book *Guilt-Free Quiet Times* helps women draw near to God. Emily loves hearing from readers at emilyeryan.com.

Noah Sanders is a farmer, homesteader, and educator who lives with his wife and eight children in rural Alabama. He is the author of *Born-Again Dirt: Farming to the Glory of God.* After running a successful small-scale farm business for over a decade, he and his family now raise much of their own food and focus on educating others in agriculture, discipleship, and missional stewardship through their ministry, redeemingthedirt.com.

Karen Sargent says she would never write devotions because she didn't feel qualified, but Jesus had different plans. Nearly ten years later, Karen has written for numerous Guideposts publications and has found her home with *Mornings with Jesus*. She is the award-winning author of *Waiting for Butterflies* and two other novels, and leads book launches for Christian authors. Karen and her husband enjoy retirement in a beautiful valley in Southeast Missouri. Visit her at karensargent.com.

After a thirty-year career in architecture, **Durwood Smith** engaged with a local writers' weekly workshop sharing daily devotionals he wrote. As such, he has published *Close Calls—a Lifeline to Jesus*. Accused of being a one-sided writer, he took up the challenge, adding detective/romance novels to his repertoire and has currently finished book two of his Jack Sinclair Mystery trilogy. Durwood enjoys living in the Seattle area.

Laura L. Smith is a best-selling author, speaker, Bible teacher, and podcaster. She tears down lies so we can live in Christ's truth. Laura lives in Oxford, Ohio, with her husband and the youngest of their four young adult kids. There you'll find her running the trails, strolling the farmers' market, or sipping a mocha at her favorite cafe. Check out Laura's latest book, *Brave Woman, Mighty God,* and visit her at laurasmithauthor.com.

Sheryl Smith-Rodgers of Blanco, Texas, has written for many state and national publications. As a Texas Master Naturalist, she gives presentations on spiders and other nature-related topics. At Window on a Texas Wildscape, she blogs about the native plant gardens that she and her husband, James Hearn, tend at their home. Her two grandchildren call her Ranea (pronounced "rainy"), which comes from the spider order of Araneae (uh-RAINY-eye). Learn more about Sheryl at sherylsmithrodgers.com.

Cindy K. Sproles is an author, speaker, and conference director. She is a cofounder and executive editor of Christian Devotions Ministries. Cindy is a freelance editor and mentor with Write Right Author Mentoring Service and has served as an acquisitions and managing editor for over ten years. Cindy, the author of six Appalachian historical novels, was born and raised in the Appalachian mountains of East Tennessee. Contact Cindy at cindyksproles@gmail.com or cindysproles.com.

Crystal Storms is an author, artist, and the calming voice behind *The Heart Rest Podcast*. With a heart to encourage, her passion is to help you release anxiety and find true peace in Christ's presence. Married to her sweetheart, Tim, since 1995, they call sunny Florida home with their adorable Yorkie, Minnie. Crystal would love to connect with you and help you find your own heart rest. Head over to crystalstorms .com and say hello!

Stephanie Thompson has loved beautiful flower beds since 1996, when she became a member of the Carefree Rose Garden Club. Back then, she had one small, empty semicircle flower bed by her front door. Decades later, she and her husband, Michael, live on two acres with more than 1,000 feet of flower beds on her property. "Tending them feels like a full-time job, but beautiful shrubs and flowers provide abundant joy," she admits.

Kit Tosello is the award-winning author of *The Color of Home*. In addition to writing big-hearted small-town novels, Kit writes for her local newspaper and has published many articles and devotions. Kit and her husband operate Suttle Tea, a loose-tea shop in central Oregon, where Kit creates artisanal tea blends enjoyed by tea aficionados across the U.S. Her favorite activities are mountain gazing, trail wandering, tea sipping, and buddy reading with grandkids. Learn more at kittosello.com.

Lawrence W. Wilson believes that God is love, life is good, and we can all be a bit better than we are now. He writes to remind people of simple truths so they will be inspired to live a better story. He lives in Indiana.

BIBLE ACKNOWLEDGMENTS

Scripture quotations marked (ESV) are taken from *The Holy Bible, English Standard Version*. Copyright © 2001 by Crossway Bibles, a division of Good News Publishers. Used by permission. All rights reserved.

Scripture quotations marked (GNT) are taken from the *Good News Translation*® (Today's English Version, Second Edition). © 1992 American Bible Society.

Scripture quotations marked (KJV) are taken from the *King James Version of the Bible*.

Scripture quotations marked (MSG) are taken from *The Message*. Copyright © 1993, 2002, 2018 by Eugene H. Peterson.

Scripture quotations marked (NASB or NASB1995) are taken from the *New American Standard Bible*®. Copyright © 1960, 1971, 1977, 1995, 2020 by The Lockman Foundation. All rights reserved.

Scripture quotations marked (NET) are taken from the *NET Bible*® (New English Translation). Copyright © 1996–2017 by Biblical Studies Press, L.L.C.; http://netbible.com. All rights reserved.

Scripture quotations marked (NIV) are taken from *The Holy Bible, New International Version*®, *NIV*®. Copyright © 1973, 1978, 1984, 2011 by Biblica, Inc. Used by permission. All rights reserved worldwide.

Scripture quotations marked (NKJV) are taken from the *New King James Version*®. Copyright © 1982 by Thomas Nelson. Used by permission. All rights reserved.

Scripture quotations marked (NLT) are taken from the *Holy Bible, New Living Translation*. Copyright © 1996, 2004, 2007, 2015 by Tyndale House Foundation. Used by permission of Tyndale House Publishers Inc., Carol Stream, Illinois. All rights reserved.

Scripture quotations marked (RSV) are taken from the *Revised Standard Version of the Bible*. Copyright © 1946, 1952, 1971 by the Division of Christian Education of the National Council of the Churches of Christ in the United States of America. Used by permission.

Scripture quotations marked (TPT) are taken from *The Passion Translation*®. Copyright © 2017, 2018, 2020 by Passion & Fire Ministries, Inc. Used by permission. All rights reserved.

A NOTE FROM THE EDITORS

We hope you enjoyed *Inspiration from the Garden*, published by Guideposts. For over 75 years, Guideposts, a nonprofit organization, has been driven by a vision of a world filled with hope. We aspire to be the voice of a trusted friend, a friend who makes you feel more hopeful and connected.

By making a purchase from Guideposts, you join our community in touching millions of lives, inspiring them to believe that all things are possible through faith, hope, and prayer. Your continued support allows us to provide uplifting resources to those in need. Whether through our communities, websites, apps, or publications, we inspire our audiences, bring them together, and comfort, uplift, entertain, and guide them. Visit us at guideposts.org to learn more.

We would love to hear from you. Write us at Guideposts, P.O. Box 5815, Harlan, Iowa 51593 or call us at (800) 932-2145. Did you love *Inspiration from the Garden*? Leave a review for this product on guideposts.org/shop. Your feedback helps others in our community find relevant products.